The Ultimate

Ninja Foodi PossibleCooker

Cookbook for Beginners

The Simple & Homemade Ninja Foodi PossibleCooker Recipes
Will Help You Cook the World's Best Food for Your Family

Gladys Roberts

Table of Contents

Introduction

The Ninja Foodi PossibleCooker PRO is an all-in-one cooking tool that provides a versatile range of functionalities to make cooking effortless and enjoyable. This cooker is designed to replace up to 14 cooking tools and appliances, including a slow cooker, pressure cooker, air fryer, and more. The PossibleCooker PRO is a convenient appliance for people who are looking for a fast and efficient way to cook their meals.

One of the most impressive features of the PossibleCooker PRO is its ability to cook up to 30% faster than a conventional oven. This means that you can prepare meals quickly and efficiently, saving you valuable time in your day. In a test on 6 lb. chickens, the PossibleCooker PRO was able to cook them faster than a conventional oven, which is an impressive feat.

The PossibleCooker PRO uses Triple Fusion Heat to combine bottom, side, and steam heating elements to provide more cooking options. This allows for even and thorough cooking of your meals, giving you the perfect results every time. This is particularly useful when you want to cook a variety of dishes, such as roasted vegetables or meats, where even cooking is essential.

The PossibleCooker PRO also has cooker-to-oven-to-table functionality, which means that you can use it to cook your meals and then transfer them directly to the table for serving. This is a convenient feature that saves you time and effort in transferring your meals from the cooker to the serving dish. Additionally, this functionality ensures that your meals stay hot and fresh when serving them to your family or guests.

The PossibleCooker PRO is an 8-in-1 cooker, which means that it has eight different functions that you can use to prepare a variety of meals. These functions include pressure cooking, slow cooking, air frying, baking, roasting, broiling, steaming, and searing. This wide range of functions allows you to prepare almost any type of meal using a single appliance, making it a versatile and valuable tool in any kitchen.

The Ninja Foodi PossibleCooker PRO is a highly versatile and efficient appliance that can replace up to 14 different cooking tools and appliances. Its Triple Fusion Heat technology and cooker-to-oven-to-table functionality make it an excellent choice for anyone who wants to prepare their meals quickly, efficiently, and with the perfect results every time. With its wide range of cooking options, the PossibleCooker PRO is a valuable addition to any kitchen, making cooking effortless and enjoyable.

The Ninja Foodi PossibleCooker PRO is a highly versatile, efficient, and valuable appliance that can replace up to 14 different cooking tools and appliances. Its Triple Fusion Heat technology and cooker-to-oven-to-table functionality make it an excellent choice for anyone who wants to prepare their meals quickly, efficiently, and with perfect results every time. Its wide range of cooking options makes it a versatile addition to any kitchen, and its efficiency makes it ideal for busy families. The PossibleCooker PRO is an excellent investment for anyone who loves cooking and wants to make their kitchen work easier and more enjoyable.

What is Ninja Foodi PossibleCooker PRO?

The Ninja Foodi PossibleCooker PRO is an all-in-one cooking appliance that is highly versatile and efficient. It can replace up to 14 different cooking tools and appliances. This makes it an excellent choice for anyone who wants to save space in their kitchen while still having access to a wide range of cooking options.

One of the standouts features of the PossibleCooker PRO is its Triple Fusion Heat technology. This technology combines bottom, side, and steam heating elements to provide even and thorough cooking. This means that your meals will be cooked perfectly every time, without any hot or cold spots. The Triple Fusion Heat technology also allows you to cook a wide range of dishes, from roasts to casseroles, with ease.

The cooker-to-oven-to-table functionality of the PossibleCooker PRO is another excellent feature that makes it a valuable addition to any kitchen. This functionality allows you to use the PossibleCooker PRO to cook your meals and then transfer them directly to the table for serving. This saves you time and effort in transferring your meals from the cooker to the serving dish, and ensures that your meals stay hot and fresh when serving them to your family or guests.

The PossibleCooker PRO also offers a wide range of cooking options, making it a versatile appliance that can handle almost any cooking task. Its functions include slow cook, bake, steam, sear/ sauté, braise, proof, sous vide and keep warm. This means that you can use the PossibleCooker PRO to prepare almost any type of meal, from breakfast to dinner and everything in between.

In addition to its versatility and functionality, the PossibleCooker PRO is also designed for efficiency. It cooks up to 30% faster than a conventional oven, which means that you can prepare your meals quickly and efficiently. This is particularly useful for busy families who want to spend less time in the kitchen and more time enjoying their meals together.

Functions of Ninja Foodi Possible- Cooker PRO

The Ninja Foodi PossibleCooker Pro comes with a variety of cooking functions that allow you to customize your cooking experience to achieve the perfect results for your favorite meals.

- Slow Cook
- Braise
- Steam
- Proof
- Sear/Sauté
- Sous Vide
- Bake
- Keep Warm

1. The **Slow Cook** function is perfect for cooking food at a lower temperature for a longer period of time, allowing flavors to meld together and resulting in deliciously tender meats and stews.

2. The **Sear/Sauté** function allows you to use the unit as a cooktop, perfect for browning meats, sautéing veggies, simmering sauces, and more. This function is great for achieving a crispy exterior on meats or vegetables before slow cooking or pressure cooking.

3. The **Braising** function is ideal for transforming tougher cuts of meat by first browning at high heat with oil and then simmering in liquid at low heat. This function is perfect for achieving fall-off-the-bone tenderness in meats.

4. The **Sous Vide** function, meaning "under vacuum" in French, is a slow cooking method that involves sealing food in a plastic bag and cooking it in a precisely regulated water bath. This function is great for achieving perfectly cooked, tender meats.

5. The **Steam** function gently cooks delicate foods at a high temperature, retaining nutrients and preserving natural flavors.

6. The **Bake** function allows you to use the unit to bake sweet and savory casseroles, bread, and desserts.

7. The **Proof** function creates an ideal environment for dough to rest and rise, perfect for homemade bread and pizza dough.

8. The **Keep Warm** function on the Ninja Foodi PossibleCooker Pro is designed to keep food warm for an extended period after it has been cooked. This feature is perfect for those who like to prepare meals ahead of time, but want to ensure that their food remains hot and fresh until it's time to serve.

By utilizing these various cooking functions, you can achieve perfect results for any meal with the Ninja Foodi PossibleCooker Pro.

Buttons guide of Ninja Foodi Possible-Cooker PRO

The Ninja Foodi PossibleCooker Pro has various operating buttons that allow you to control and customize your cooking experience.

The power button: The Power button is located at the top of the unit and is used to turn the unit on and off, stopping all cooking modes.

The temp arrow: The temperature arrows, located to the left of the display, can be used to adjust the cooking temperature. Simply press the up or down arrow until you reach your desired temperature.

The time arrow: The time arrows, located to the right of the display, can be used to adjust the cooking time. Press the up or down arrow until you reach your desired time.

The Start/Stop button: The Start/Stop button is used to initiate the cooking process. Press the START button to begin cooking. If you need to stop the cooking process at any time, simply press the START/STOP button during the cook cycle.

The Function Dial: The Function Dial is located on the front of the unit and allows you to select a cook function. Simply turn the dial to the desired function, such as slow cook, bake, sear/sauté, or steam. Each function is clearly labeled on the dial for easy selection.

By utilizing these operating buttons

and the Function Dial, you can easily control the temperature, time, and cook function to create delicious and healthy meals for you and your loved ones with the Ninja Foodi PossibleCooker Pro.

Parts and Accessories of Ninja Foodi PossibleCooker PRO

The Ninja Foodi PossibleCooker PRO has various accessories to make cooking easier. When you purchase the Ninja Foodi PossibleCooker PRO, you'll receive the following items:

- Spoon-Ladle
- Top Pot Handle/Spoon-Ladle Rest
- Cooking Lid
- Side Pot Handles
- 8.5-Quart Cooking Pot
- Side Pot Handles
- Main Unit
- Control Panel

Before First Use

Before using the PossibleCooker Pro, it is important to follow these simple steps to ensure proper operation and

avoid any potential damage or injury:

1. Remove any packaging material, stickers, and tape from the unit and discard them appropriately.

2. Take all accessories out of the packaging and read the manual carefully, paying close attention to operational instructions, warnings, and important safeguards.

3. Wash the Main Base Unit, Inner cooking pot, cooking pot lid, and Spoon–ladle with a damp, soapy cloth. Rinse with a clean damp cloth and dry thoroughly. Do not submerge the main unit in water.

4. It is recommended to turn on the unit and let it run for 10 minutes without adding food to remove any packaging residue and odor traces. Ensure the area is well ventilated. This process is completely safe and does not affect the performance of the PossibleCooker Pro.

Step-By-Step Using Ninja Foodi

PossibleCooker PRO

Slow Cook

1. To begin slow cooking, first, use the dial to choose the SLOW COOK option. Then, use the +/- TEMP arrows to select either HI or LO. After that, select a cook time between 3 and 12 hours in 15-minute increments, and press the START/STOP button to begin cooking.

2. Once the cook time reaches zero, the unit will beep and automatically switch to the KEEP WARM setting, and start counting up. You can adjust the SLOW COOK LO time between 6 and 12 hours, and the SLOW COOK HI time can be adjusted between 3 and 12 hours.

Sear/Sauté

1. To start SEAR/SAUTE function, rotate the dial and select it. Then, use the +/- TEMP buttons to set the temperature to either HI or LO as per your preference. Wait for the unit to heat up for about 5 minutes before adding any ingredients.

2. To begin cooking, press the START/STOP button. Conversely, to turn off the SEAR/SAUTE function, press the START/STOP button again. Finally, if there is steam, take necessary precautions.

Braise

1. To prepare for BRAISING, start by following the Sear/Sauté instructions to sear the ingredients in the pot. Once that is complete, deglaze the pot by pouring wine or stock and scraping the brown bits from the

bottom of the pot into the cooking liquid.

2. Next, add the remaining cooking liquid and ingredients into the pot. Turn the dial to select BRAISE, and the default temperature setting will be displayed.

3. Set the cook time in 15-minute increments using the +/- TIME arrows. Once you have set the time, press the START/STOP button to begin cooking.

4. If you need to deglaze the pot, pour 1 cup of liquid into the pot, scrape the brown bits from the bottom, and mix them into the cooking liquid.

Sous Vide

1. To prepare for SOUS VIDE cooking, first, pour 12 cups of room-temperature water into the pot. Next, close the lid and turn the dial to SOUS VIDE. The default temperature will be displayed. Use the TEMP arrows to set the temperature in 5-degree increments

between 120°F and 190°F.

2. The cook time will default to 3 hours. To adjust the cook time, use the TIME arrows. You can adjust the time in 15-minute increments up to 12 hours, or in 1-hour increments from 12 to 24 hours.

3. Press the START/STOP button to begin cooking. The unit display will flash between "PrE" and the current temperature, indicating that preheating is in progress. Once preheating is complete, "ADD FOOD" will flash on the display. After 30 seconds, the unit will start counting down from the preset cook time.

Steam

1. To initiate STEAM cooking, turn the dial and choose STEAM option. Then, use the +/- TIME arrows to set the cook time, adjusting it in 1-minute increments as per your requirements.

2. Press the START/STOP button to start the cooking process. The display will show "PrE," indicating that the unit is preheating to the selected temperature.

3. When the unit reaches the appropriate steam level, the display will show the set temperature, and the timer will begin counting down. Once the cook time reaches zero, the unit will beep,

and "END" will be displayed.

Bake

1. To start baking, first, place the ingredients into the pot. Turn the dial to select BAKE, and the default temperature will be displayed.

2. Use the +/- TEMP arrows to set the temperature between 250°F and 425°F. You can adjust the cook time using the +/- TIME arrows. You can adjust the time in 1-minute increments up to 1 hour, or in 5-minute increments up to 6 hours.

3. Press the START/STOP button to begin cooking. When the cook time reaches zero, the unit will beep, and the display will show END for 5 minutes. If the food requires more time, use the +/- TIME arrows to add more time.

Proof

1. To proof your dough, place it into the pot and put the lid on top. Then, turn the dial to select PROOF, and the default temperature setting will be displayed.

2. Use the +/- TEMP arrows to set the temperature in 5-degree increments between 90°F and 105°F. You can adjust the proof time using the +/- TIME arrows in 5-minute increments.

3. Press the START/STOP button to begin cooking. When the proof time reaches zero, the unit will beep, and END will flash 3 times on the display.

Keep Warm

1. To activate the KEEP WARM function, turn the dial to select it. The temperature will automatically default, and the unit will start counting up.

2. To adjust the cook time, use the +/- TIME arrows. You can adjust the time in 1-minute increments for up to 1 hour, or in 5-minute increments for up to 6 hours.

Tips for Using Accessories

Here are some tips for using the accessories with the Ninja Foodi PossibleCooker Pro:

Spoon-Ladle:

- Use the spoon-ladle for serving food or stirring ingredients in the pot.
- Place the spoon-ladle in the top pot handle/spoon-ladle rest when not in

use.

Top Pot Handle/Spoon-Ladle Rest:

- Use the top pot handle to lift the cooking pot out of the main unit.
- Use the spoon-ladle rest to keep the spoon-ladle within reach while cooking.

Cooking Lid:

- Use the cooking lid to cover the cooking pot during the cooking process.
- The cooking lid has a steam vent to release excess steam during cooking.

Side Pot Handles:

- Use the side pot handles to lift the cooking pot in and out of the main unit.
- The side pot handles make it easy to transport the cooking pot to the table for serving.

8.5-Quart Cooking Pot:

- The 8.5-quart cooking pot is the main cooking vessel for the Ninja Foodi PossibleCooker Pro.
- It is oven-safe up to 500°F, making it versatile for many different cooking methods.

Main Unit:

- The main unit houses the heating element and controls for the Ninja Foodi PossibleCooker Pro.
- Use the control panel to select cooking

functions and adjust temperature and time settings.

Control Panel:

- The control panel allows you to select cooking functions and adjust temperature and time settings.
- The panel also displays error messages and notifications, such as when the cooking pot or water level is not detected.

Benefits of Ninja Foodi PossibleCooker Pro

The Ninja Foodi PossibleCooker Pro is a versatile kitchen appliance that offers several benefits, including:

- **Multi-functionality:** The PossibleCooker Pro can pressure cook, slow cook, steam, bake, roast, broil, dehydrate, and air fry all in one appliance, making it a great addition to any kitchen.
- **Time-saving:** With the PossibleCooker Pro, you can cook meals up to 70% faster than traditional cooking

methods, which can save you time in the kitchen.

- **Healthier cooking:** The air fryer function allows you to enjoy crispy foods without the excess oil, which can help you to prepare healthier meals.
- **Large capacity:** The 8.5-quart cooking pot allows you to cook large meals or batch cook for meal prep, making it a great choice for families or those who like to entertain.
- **Easy to use:** The PossibleCooker Pro features a user-friendly control panel with preset cooking functions, making it easy to use even if you're not an experienced cook.
- **Easy to clean:** The non-stick cooking pot and accessories are dishwasher safe, and the main unit can be easily wiped down with a damp cloth.
- You can cook frozen food directly in the PossibleCooker PRO without thawing, and the results will be perfect.
- The PossibleCooker PRO consumes less energy than a conventional oven, making it an energy-efficient option for your kitchen.
- If you're hosting a BBQ party, the PossibleCooker PRO is an ideal choice as it allows you to manage the

cooking without generating smoke or igniting a fire.

- With its user-friendly interface, you can easily operate the PossibleCooker PRO. Just place your food inside and select the function you want, and the appliance will do the rest.

- The PossibleCooker PRO is an excellent kitchen appliance for health-conscious individuals as its ceramic-coated grate prevents food from sticking, ensuring perfect and healthy meals every time.

- The PossibleCooker PRO is a multipurpose appliance that replaces the need for multiple appliances, helping you save money while adding versatility to your cooking routine.

- Whether you're a beginner or an experienced cook, the PossibleCooker PRO allows you to cook your favorite dishes to perfection every time.

- With the PossibleCooker PRO, you can enjoy perfectly cooked tender meats, crispy roasts, and vegetables anytime you want, with consistent quality and results.

- The Ninja Foodi PossibleCooker Pro is perfect for BBQ parties as it enables you to cook without smoke or the risk of a fire.

- With its intuitive interface, operating

the Ninja Foodi PossibleCooker Pro is a breeze. Just add your ingredients and select the desired function, and the appliance will take care of the rest. Overall, the Ninja Foodi PossibleCooker Pro offers a range of benefits that can make meal prep and cooking easier, faster, and healthier.

Cleaning and Caring for Ninja Foodi PossibleCooker PRO

The unit must be cleaned thoroughly after each use.

1. Before cleaning, unplug the unit from the wall outlet.
2. To clean the cooker base and control panel, wipe them with a damp cloth.
3. It is recommended to wash the cooking pot by hand to extend its life. If there is any food residue stuck on the cooking pot, fill the pot with water and allow it to soak before cleaning. Do not use scouring pads. If scrubbing is necessary, use a non-abrasive

cleanser or liquid dish soap with a nylon pad or brush.

4. The glass lid and spoon-ladle can be washed in the dishwasher. If there is any food residue stuck on the glass lid or spoon-ladle, use a non-abrasive cleanser.

5. After cleaning, air-dry all parts.

1. The inner cooking pot is safe to use in ovens with temperatures up to 500°F.

2. To keep food at a warm and safe temperature after cooking, use the Keep Warm mode.

3. Avoid removing the lid during the cooking cycle.

4. The Cooking Pot should not be used on stove tops.

5. The glass lid can be washed in the dishwasher.

6. The Spoon-ladle is dishwasher safe.

7. The preheat time will vary depending on the temperature and quantity of the ingredients.

8. Always wear oven mitts when removing the cooking pot from the base unit.

9. Always wear oven mitts when removing the glass lid from the cooking pot.

10. Store extra food in containers that are freezer-friendly and sealed.

11. The bake function is suitable for cooking food with high water content, such as casseroles, cobblers, and deep-dish desserts.

Frequently Asked Questions & Notes

If your Ninja Foodi possible cooker Pro is not turning on?

● Ensure that the power cord is securely plugged into the outlet.

● Try plugging the cord into a different outlet to eliminate the possibility of a faulty outlet.

● Reset the circuit breaker if necessary to rule out a tripped breaker as the cause of the issue.

"ADD POT" error message may appear on the display screen?

If the cooking pot is not inside the cooker base. Please ensure that the cooking pot is properly placed inside the cooker base before attempting to use any

function. The cooking pot is required for all functions to work properly.

If the Ninja Foodi Possible Cooker Pro displays an "ADD WATER" error message on the screen?

It means that the water level in the unit is too low. To continue cooking, more water should be added to the cooking pot.

Timer is slow?

If you find that the time is counting down too slowly on your Ninja Foodi PossibleCooker Pro, it's possible that you may have accidentally set the timer for hours instead of minutes. Remember that when setting the time, the display will show the hours and minutes as "HH:MM" and the time will increase or decrease in one-minute increments.

"E1" or "E2" Error?

If you see the error codes "E1" or "E2" on the display screen:

It indicates that there is a problem with the unit's functionality. Please reach out to Customer Service at 1-877-646-5288. We recommend registering your product online at registeryourninja.com before calling, and have the product with you so that we can assist you better.

4-Week Meal Plan

Week 1

Day 1:
Breakfast: Breakfast Apple Oatmeal
Lunch: Potato Cheese Tacos
Snack: Candied Almonds
Dinner: Spicy Cheese Chicken & Tortilla Chips Casserole
Dessert: Curried Fruit Granola

Day 2:
Breakfast: Cheesy Spinach and Egg Casserole
Lunch: Vegetarian Curry with Wild Rice
Snack: Yummy Oriental Snack Mix
Dinner: Herbed Beef and Spaghetti
Dessert: Red Wine-Poached Pears

Day 3:
Breakfast: Sweet Potato Casserole with Pecans & Bacon
Lunch: Cheesy Summer Vegetables Lasagna
Snack: Lemony Hummus
Dinner: Cheesy Bacon-Wrapped Chicken Stew
Dessert: Caramel Cream Marshmallow Fondue

Day 4:
Breakfast: Sweet Sausage Rolls
Lunch: Acorn Squash & Chickpea Stew over Couscous
Snack: Rice and Meat Stuffed Grape Leaves
Dinner: Swiss Steak and Carrot
Dessert: Fruit Bread Pudding

Day 5:
Breakfast: Cheese Egg Pitas
Lunch: Creamy Cheesy Potatoes Casserole
Snack: Crispy Coconut Chicken Fingers
Dinner: Chicken and Pineapple Curry
Dessert: Tasty Chocolate Coconut Peanut Clusters

Day 6:
Breakfast: Cheesy Breakfast Sausage Casserole
Lunch: Spicy Corn Bread
Snack: Bell Pepper & Olive Salad with Maple-Mustard Dressing
Dinner: Pot Roast with Potato & Carrot
Dessert: Banana Apple Smoothie

Day 7:
Breakfast: Delicious Smoked Salmon & Potato Casserole
Lunch: Honey-Mustard Glazed Carrots
Snack: Savory Veggie Pot Stuffing
Dinner: Turkey and Squash Stew
Dessert: Minty Cabbage & Grape Smoothie

Week 2

Day 1:
Breakfast: Rosemary Prosciutto and Potato Breakfast Casserole
Lunch: Eggplant Parmesan with Almonds
Snack: Spicy Red Beans and Rice Casserole
Dinner: Lime Chicken and Brown Rice Casserole
Dessert: Lemony Dessert Peaches

Day 2:
Breakfast: Sausage, Broccoli & Sweet Potato Casserole
Lunch: Juicy Cranberry-Walnut and Green Beans
Snack: Gingered Rice and Veggie Pilaf with Apricot
Dinner: Sweet & Sour Beef with Green Beans
Dessert: Pineapple Carrot Cake

Day 3:
Breakfast: Cinnamon-Raisin Breakfast Toast
Lunch: Spiced Cauliflower, Potatoes, & Peas
Snack: Hoisin-Honey Glazed Chicken Wings
Dinner: Sweet and Sour Pork Chops with Cabbage
Dessert: Delicious Banana Foster

Day 4:
Breakfast: Banana and Walnuts Oatmeal
Lunch: Juicy Beets
Snack: Cheese-Beer Fondue
Dinner: Chipotle-Peanut Butter Chicken and Potatoes
Dessert: Chocolate Brownie Cake

Day 5:
Breakfast: Apple-Raisins Steel-Cut Oats
Lunch: Cauliflower Curry with Peas
Snack: Classic Caponata
Dinner: Cumin Pulled Pork
Dessert: Vanilla Almond-Caramel Sauce

Day 6:
Breakfast: Caramel Peach Steel-Cut Oats
Lunch: Lemony Rosemary Fingerling Potatoes
Snack: Spiced Cranberry-Apple Cider
Dinner: Pork Chops with Apricot and Carrot
Dessert: Pumpkin-Cranberry Bread Pudding

Day 7:
Breakfast: Breakfast French Toast with Berries
Lunch: Orange-Soy Kale and Mushroom Salad
Snack: Simple Candied Pecans
Dinner: Chicken Caesar Pasta
Dessert: Honey Bananas

Week 3

Day 1:
Breakfast: Apple and Almonds French Toast Casserole
Lunch: Rice and Apple Stuffed Acorn Squash
Snack: Balsamic Brussels Sprouts and Cranberry
Dinner: Juicy Pork Roast with Raisins
Dessert: Homemade Peanut Butter Chocolate Cake

Day 2:
Breakfast: Quinoa, Oats and Apple Casserole
Lunch: Sweet Potato Hash with Nuts
Snack: Sweet Carrots and Peppers
Dinner: Simple Salsa Chicken
Dessert: Vanilla Chocolate Lava Cake

Day 3:
Breakfast: Breakfast Apple Oatmeal
Lunch: Sweet & Sour Pulled Jackfruit
Snack: Spiced Mixed Nuts
Dinner: Balsamic Beef with Red Cabbage
Dessert: Pumpkin Cake

Day 4:
Breakfast: Cheesy Spinach and Egg Casserole
Lunch: Cheese Tofu and Mushroom Enchiladas
Snack: Juicy Honey-Soy Chicken Wings
Dinner: Lemony Chicken Stew
Dessert: Cherries Stuffed Apples

Day 5:
Breakfast: Sweet Potato Casserole with Pecans & Bacon
Lunch: Spicy No-Cheese Enchilada Casserole
Snack: Spiced Nuts
Dinner: Red Wine-Braised Beef Brisket
Dessert: Peach Crumble

Day 6:
Breakfast: Sweet Sausage Rolls
Lunch: Healthy Quinoa Tacos
Snack: Creamy French Onion Dip
Dinner: Herbed Chicken Thighs with Grape Tomatoes
Dessert: Cinnamon Oranges with Raspberries

Day 7:
Breakfast: Cheese Egg Pitas
Lunch: Beans and Corns Enchilada Casserole
Snack: Lemony Spinach and Artichoke Dip
Dinner: Spiced Beef Roast with Mushrooms & Celery
Dessert: Baked Five-Spice Stuffed Apples

Week 4

Day 1:
Breakfast: Cheesy Breakfast Sausage Casserole
Lunch: Vegetarian Curry with Wild Rice
Snack: Candied Almonds
Dinner: Lemony Lamb Shoulder with Red Potatoes
Dessert: Curried Fruit Granola

Day 2:
Breakfast: Delicious Smoked Salmon & Potato Casserole
Lunch: Cheesy Summer Vegetables Lasagna
Snack: Yummy Oriental Snack Mix
Dinner: Turkey Sausage with Red Beans & Brown Rice
Dessert: Red Wine-Poached Pears

Day 3:
Breakfast: Rosemary Prosciutto and Potato Breakfast Casserole
Lunch: Acorn Squash & Chickpea Stew over Couscous
Snack: Lemony Hummus
Dinner: Spanish-Style Lamb Chops with Red Potatoes
Dessert: Caramel Cream Marshmallow Fondue

Day 4:
Breakfast: Sausage, Broccoli & Sweet Potato Casserole
Lunch: Creamy Cheesy Potatoes Casserole
Snack: Rice and Meat Stuffed Grape Leaves
Dinner: Smoky Pork Stew with White Hominy
Dessert: Fruit Bread Pudding

Day 5:
Breakfast: Cinnamon-Raisin Breakfast Toast
Lunch: Honey-Mustard Glazed Carrots
Snack: Crispy Coconut Chicken Fingers
Dinner: Beef Stew with Chopped Veggies & Olives
Dessert: Tasty Chocolate Coconut Peanut Clusters

Day 6:
Breakfast: Banana and Walnuts Oatmeal
Lunch: Eggplant Parmesan with Almonds
Snack: Bell Pepper & Olive Salad with Maple-Mustard Dressing
Dinner: Curried Brown Rice with Ground Lamb
Dessert: Banana Apple Smoothie

Day 7:
Breakfast: Apple-Raisins Steel-Cut Oats
Lunch: Juicy Cranberry-Walnut and Green Beans
Snack: Spicy Red Beans and Rice Casserole
Dinner: Balsamic Pork Tenderloin with Peach Sauce
Dessert: Minty Cabbage & Grape Smoothie

Chapter 1 Breakfast Recipes

Breakfast Apple Oatmeal

Prep time: 10 minutes | **Cook time:** 7-9 hours | **Serves:** 8

2 cups steel-cut oats	2 apples, peeled and chopped
5 cups water	½ cup dried fruit bits
1½ cups orange juice	½ cup brown sugar
½ teaspoon salt	½ cup half-and-half
½ teaspoon cinnamon	1 cup granola

1. Toast the oats the night before you plan to eat by cooking them over low heat in a small saucepan for 5-8 minutes, stirring regularly until they become a light golden brown color. Then, put the toasted oats in the pot. 2. Add remaining ingredients except half-and-half and granola to the pot. Stir well. Cover with the lid. Turn dial to Slow Cook, cook on low heat for 7–9 hours. 3. In the morning, stir in the half-and-half and cook on Slow Cook function for 10 minutes longer. Sprinkle with granola and serve.

Per Serving: Calories 196; Fat 3. 09g; Sodium 177mg; Carbs 46. 98g; Fiber 5. 2g; Sugar 26. 62g; Protein 5. 3g

Cheesy Spinach and Egg Casserole

Prep time: 10 minutes | **Cook time:** 5-6 hours | **Serves:** 6

1 (16-ounce) bag frozen cut leaf spinach	½ teaspoon salt
2 cups cottage cheese	½ teaspoon dried basil leaves
1 (3-ounce) package cream cheese	⅛ teaspoon pepper
1 cup shredded Cheddar cheese, divided	4 tablespoons butter, melted
4 eggs, beaten	1 tablespoon chopped parsley
¼ cup flour	

1. Firstly, defrost the spinach and remove any excess water before adding it to a big bowl. Then, use a food processor to combine cream cheese and cottage cheese until the mixture is smooth. Add the cheese mixture to the spinach along with half a cup of Cheddar cheese. 2. In a separate small bowl, mix and beat the eggs, flour, salt, basil, pepper, and butter until well combined. Then, add this mixture to the spinach and cheese mixture and stir everything together. 3. Pour into the pot. Cover with the lid and turn dial to Slow Cook, cook on low heat for 5–6 hours or until mixture is set. 4. Sprinkle with ¼ cup Cheddar cheese and parsley; cover, and let stand until cheese is melted. Serve right away.

Per Serving: Calories 378; Fat 28. 13g; Sodium 803mg; Carbs 10. 16g; Fiber 1. 7g; Sugar 3. 3g; Protein 21. 92g

Sweet Potato Casserole with Pecans & Bacon

Prep time: 10 minutes | **Cook time:** 8½–9½ hours | **Serves:** 4

4 slices bacon	¼ cup applesauce
1 onion, chopped	3 tablespoons butter, melted
3 sweet potatoes, peeled	½ teaspoon salt
⅓ cup brown sugar	⅛ teaspoon pepper
¼ cup orange juice	¼ cup chopped pecans

1. Place bacon in the pot. Turn dial to Sear/Sauté, set temperature to LO, and press START/STOP to begin cooking, about 3 minutes until the bacon is crisp. 2. After draining on paper towels, crumble the bacon and keep the crumbled mixture in the refrigerator. 3. Remove most of the drippings from the pot, leaving only 2 tablespoons. 4. Add onion to the pot and stir for 5 minutes until it softens, while scraping any brown bits from the pot. 5. Cut sweet potatoes into 1-inch cubes and mix them with the onions in the pot. 6. In a small bowl, combine all remaining ingredients except pecans and stir well. Pour into the pot. 7. Cover with the lid. Turn dial to Slow Cook and cook on low heat for 8–9 hours or until potatoes are tender. 8. When the unit beeps, remove the lid and Stir in reserved bacon and the pecans; cover and cook for 30 minutes longer. If desired, you can place a fried egg on top of each serving of hash.

Per Serving: Calories 507; Fat 23. 72g; Sodium 490mg; Carbs 68. 7g; Fiber 7. 4g; Sugar 36. 17g; Protein 7. 77g

Sweet Sausage Rolls

Prep time: 10 minutes | **Cook time:** 8 hours | **Serves:** 8

¾ cup soft bread crumbs	½ teaspoon dried marjoram leaves
1 egg, beaten	1½-pounds mild bulk pork sausage
¼ cup brown sugar	2 tablespoons butter
¼ cup applesauce	¼ cup honey
½ teaspoon salt	¼ cup chicken broth
⅛ teaspoon pepper	

1. Mix together the crumbs, egg, brown sugar, applesauce, salt, pepper, and marjoram in a large bowl. Stir well and add the sausage. 2. Shape the mixture into 3" × 1" rolls. Use the dial to select Sear/Sauté. Press the +/- TEMP buttons to choose LO temperature, press START/STOP to begin cooking. Add the butter to the pot and heat it until melted. Then, add sausage rolls, about 8 at a time, and cook until browned on all sides, about 5–6 minutes. 3. In a small bowl, combine honey and chicken broth and mix well. Pour over sausage rolls in the pot. 4. Cover with lid. Turn dial to Slow Cook, set temperature to LO, and set time to 8 hours. Press START/STOP to begin cooking. 5. When cooking is complete, remove from the pot with slotted spoon to serve.

Per Serving: Calories 401; Fat 27. 9g; Sodium 923mg; Carbs 19. 45g; Fiber 0. 2g; Sugar 17. 33g; Protein 18. 9g

Cheese Egg Pitas

Prep time: 10 minutes | **Cook time:** 7-8 hours | **Serves:** 4

2 tablespoons butter	⅛ teaspoon pepper
1 onion, chopped	½ cup salsa
2 cloves garlic, chopped	1 cup shredded pepper jack cheese
8 eggs, beaten	4 pita breads
½ teaspoon salt	2 tablespoons chopped parsley

1. The night before, spray the pot of your Ninja Foodi Possible Cooker with nonstick cooking spray. 2. Add the butter to the pot. Use the dial to select Sear/Sauté. Press the +/- TEMP buttons to choose LO temperature, press START/STOP to begin cooking. Once the butter is melted, add the onion and garlic, cook until tender, stir frequently, about 5 minutes. Press START/STOP to turn off the SEAR/SAUTE function. Open the lid and stir in salsa and cheese. 3. In large bowl, combine eggs, salt, and pepper and beat well. Pour into the pot. Cover with the lid. Turn dial to Slow Cook and cook on low heat for 7–8 hours. 4. In the morning, stir mixture in the pot. Split pita breads and fill with egg mixture; top with parsley and serve right away.

Per Serving: Calories 519; Fat 34. 3g; Sodium 1093mg; Carbs 23. 6g; Fiber 1. 8g; Sugar 4. 37g; Protein 28. 34g

Cheesy Breakfast Sausage Casserole

Prep time: 10 minutes | **Cook time:** 4-5 hours | **Serves:** 5

½ pound breakfast link sausage	½ cup whole milk
5 slices cracked wheat bread, cubed	½ cup small-curd cottage cheese
1 red bell pepper, chopped	1 tablespoon yellow mustard
½ cup shredded Swiss cheese	½ teaspoon salt
½ cup shredded Muenster cheese	⅛ teaspoon white pepper
4 eggs	¼ cup shredded Romano cheese

1. Place the sausage in the pot and cover with the lid. Use the dial to select SEAR/SAUTE. Press the +/- TEMP buttons to choose LO temperature. Press START/STOP to begin cooking. Allow it to cook for 3 minutes. Once done, remove the sausage from the pot and drain on paper towels, then cut into 1-inch pieces. Spray the pot with nonstick cooking spray. 2. Layer sausage pieces, bread, bell pepper, and Swiss and Muenster cheeses in the pot. 3. In a food processor, combine eggs, milk, cottage cheese, mustard, salt, and white pepper. Process until smooth. Pour into the pot. Let stand for 20 minutes. 4. Sprinkle with Romano cheese; cover with the lid. Turn dial to Slow Cook and cook on high for 3 hours, then reduce heat to low and cook for another 1 to 1½ hours or until casserole is set.

Per Serving: Calories 440; Fat 26. 67g; Sodium 986mg; Carbs 21. 42g; Fiber 1. 4g; Sugar 6. 77g; Protein 27. 72g

Delicious Smoked Salmon & Potato Casserole

Prep time: 10 minutes | **Cook time:** 8 hours | **Serves:** 4

1 teaspoon butter, at room temperature, or extra-virgin olive oil	⅛ teaspoon sea salt
2 eggs	Freshly ground black pepper
1 cup 2% milk	2 medium russet potatoes, peeled and sliced thin
1 teaspoon dried dill	4 ounces smoked salmon

1. Grease the inside of the pot with the butter. 2. In a small bowl, mix together the eggs, dill, milk, salt, and a few grinds of the black pepper. 3. Spread one-third of the potatoes in a single layer on the bottom of the pot and top with one-third of the salmon. Pour one-third of the egg mixture over the salmon. Repeat this layering with the remaining potatoes, salmon, and egg mixture. 4. Cover and turn dial to Slow Cook, cook on low for 8 hours or overnight.

Per Serving: Calories 301; Fat 10. 03g; Sodium 295mg; Carbs 37. 15g; Fiber 2. 5g; Sugar 4. 55g; Protein 16. 31g

Rosemary Prosciutto and Potato Breakfast Casserole

Prep time: 10 minutes | **Cook time:** 8 hours | **Serves:** 4

1 teaspoon butter, at room temperature, or extra-virgin olive oil	⅛ teaspoon sea salt
4 eggs	Freshly ground black pepper
½ cup 2% milk	2 medium russet potatoes, peeled and sliced thin
1 tablespoon minced fresh rosemary	2 ounces prosciutto

1. Grease the inside of the pot with the butter. 2. In a small bowl, combine the eggs, rosemary, milk, salt, and a few grinds of the black pepper, mix well. 3. Layer one-third of the potatoes in bottom of the pot and top with one-third of the prosciutto. Pour one-third of the egg mixture over the prosciutto. Repeat this layering with the remaining ingredients. 4. Cover with the lid and Turn dial to Slow Cook, cook on low heat for 8 hours or overnight.

Per Serving: Calories 352; Fat 15. 63g; Sodium 381mg; Carbs 36. 51g; Fiber 2. 5g; Sugar 3. 46g; Protein 16. 61g

Sausage, Broccoli & Sweet Potato Casserole

Prep time: 15 minutes | **Cook time:** 4-5 hours | **Serves:** 4

8 ounces bulk chicken or turkey sausage	1 teaspoon garlic powder
1 tablespoon unsalted butter, at room temperature	⅛ teaspoon freshly ground black pepper
6 large eggs	2 cups broccoli florets
½ cup 2% milk	1 medium onion, diced
2 teaspoons Dijon mustard	1 cup diced canned, drained sweet potato
½ teaspoon sea salt	

1. Add the sausage to the pot. Turn dial to Sear/Sauté, set temperature to LO, and press START/STOP to begin cooking. Stirring with a wooden spoon to break up the meat, for 7 to 8 minutes, until cooked through. Press START/STOP to turn off the Sear/Sauté function. Transfer to a plate and drain if necessary, set aside. 2. Grease the pot with the butter. 3. Combine eggs, milk, garlic powder, mustard, salt, and pepper in a medium bowl using a whisk. 4. Put broccoli, onion, sweet potato, and cooked sausage (that has been drained) into the pot. Then, pour the egg mixture over the top of the other ingredients, making sure they are completely covered. 5. Cover and Turn dial to Slow Cook, set temperature to LO, cook for 4 to 5 hours, until the eggs are set and the vegetables are tender, or until a food thermometer registers 160°F. Serve.

Per Serving: Calories 365; Fat 23. 11g; Sodium 870mg; Carbs 19. 09g; Fiber 2. 7g; Sugar 5. 78g; Protein 19. 78g

Cinnamon–Raisin Breakfast Toast

Prep time: 10 minutes | **Cook time:** 2 hours | **Serves:** 6

1 tablespoon unsalted butter, at room temperature	1 cup 2% milk
1 loaf cinnamon-raisin bread, cut into 1-inch cubes	1 tablespoon pure vanilla extract
6 large eggs	1 teaspoon ground cinnamon

1. Grease the pot with the butter. Place the bread cubes in the pot. 2. Combine the eggs, milk, vanilla extract, and cinnamon in a bowl. Pour the egg mixture over the bread, making sure all the bread is soaked in the mixture. 3. Cover with the lid. Turn dial to Slow Cook and cook on high for 2 hours, or until the mixture is puffed and a food thermometer inserted into the center registers 165°F.

Per Serving: Calories 99; Fat 7. 13g; Sodium 27mg; Carbs 3. 24g; Fiber 0. 2g; Sugar 2. 48g; Protein 4. 08g

Banana and Walnuts Oatmeal

Prep time: 10 minutes | Cook time: 8 hours | Serves: 6

1 tablespoon butter, plus more for serving
2 cups oats
2 bananas, mashed
½ cup finely chopped walnuts
1 teaspoon ground cinnamon

¼ teaspoon sea salt
6 cups water
1 cup whole milk or dairy-free milk, for serving
Brown sugar, for serving

1. Coat the interior of the pot with the butter. 2. Add the oats, walnuts, bananas, cinnamon, salt, and water to the pot, stir well. 3. Cover with the lid, turn dial to Slow Cook and cook on low heat for 8 hours. Serve with the milk, additional butter, and brown sugar.

Per Serving: Calories 213; Fat 8. 83g; Sodium 141mg; Carbs 40. 02g; Fiber 6. 5g; Sugar 14. 47g; Protein 7. 88g

Apple–Raisins Steel–Cut Oats

Prep time: 10 minutes | Cook time: 8 hours | Serves: 6

1 tablespoon butter, plus more for serving
2 cups steel-cut oats
2 apples, peeled, cored, and diced
1 cup raisins
1 cup apple juice

2 teaspoons ground cinnamon
¼ teaspoon sea salt
2 tablespoons brown sugar, plus more for serving
3 cups water

1. Coat the interior of the pot with the butter. 2. Add oats, raisins, apples, brown sugar, apple juice, cinnamon, salt, and water to the pot. Stir gently to mix. 3. Cover with the lid and turn dial to Slow Cook, cook on low for 8 hours. Serve hot with additional butter and brown sugar.

Per Serving: Calories 157; Fat 4. 29g; Sodium 118mg; Carbs 37. 22g; Fiber 6. 8g; Sugar 13. 41g; Protein 5. 68g

Caramel Peach Steel–Cut Oats

Prep time: 10 minutes | **Cook time:** 8 hours | **Serves:** 6

1 tablespoon butter, plus more for serving	½ cup brown sugar
2 cups steel-cut oats	1 tablespoon vanilla extract
2 peaches, peeled, pitted, and sliced	1 teaspoon sea salt
½ cup heavy (whipping) cream	4 cups water

1. Coat the interior of the pot with the butter, making sure to cover about two-thirds up the sides of the pot. 2. Add oats, peaches, vanilla, brown sugar, salt, cream, and water to the pot. Stir gently to mix. 3. Cover with the lid and turn dial to Slow Cook, cook on low for 8 hours. Serve with additional butter.

Per Serving: Calories 209; Fat 7. 83g; Sodium 417mg; Carbs 40. 53g; Fiber 4. 9g; Sugar 19. 94g; Protein 5. 7g

Breakfast French Toast with Berries

Prep time: 10 minutes | **Cook time:** 2 hours | **Serves:** 6

1 tablespoon butter, plus more for serving	1 loaf artisan white bread, cut into 2-inch pieces
2 cups whole milk	2 (6-ounce) containers mixed berries, such as
6 large eggs	blueberries, raspberries, and strawberries
1 tablespoon vanilla extract	Maple syrup, for serving
½ teaspoon ground cinnamon	

1. Coat the inside of the pot with the butter. 2. Add the milk, eggs, vanilla, and cinnamon to a bowl and mix well. 3. Put the bread and berries in the pot and pour the egg mixture over the top. Gently tap the pot on the countertop to ensure the egg mixture settles into any air pockets. 4. Cover with the lid and turn dial to Slow Cook, cook on high for 2 hours. Serve with additional butter and the maple syrup.

Per Serving: Calories 320; Fat 11. 19g; Sodium 252mg; Carbs 45. 33g; Fiber 3. 2g; Sugar 27. 29g; Protein 8. 92g

Apple and Almonds French Toast Casserole

Prep time: 15 minutes | **Cook time:** 7 hours | **Serves:** 6

For the Filling:

2 tablespoons honey

½ cup low-fat ricotta cheese

⅓ cup sliced almonds

½ teaspoon cinnamon

3 cups finely diced apples pieces

For the French Toast:

Cooking spray

2 eggs

2 egg whites

1½ cups nonfat milk (or almond or soy milk)

1 tablespoon honey

1 teaspoon vanilla extract

½ teaspoon cinnamon

12 slices light whole-grain bread, lightly toasted

To make the filling: 1. In a big bowl, combine the honey, ricotta cheese, almonds, and cinnamon until uniform. 2. Add the apples and stir to coat.

To make the French toast: 1. Spray the inside of the pot with nonstick cooking spray. 2. Combine the eggs, egg whites, honey, vanilla, milk, and cinnamon in a medium bowl. 3. Cut the toasted bread into 1-inch squares. Place ⅓ of the bread in the bottom of the pot. Top with ⅓ of the filling mixture. Repeat twice with the remaining bread and apple mixture. 4. Pour the egg mixture over the contents of the pot. Cover, turn dial to Slow Cook and cook on high for 2 to 2½ hours, or on low for 7 hours, until set.

Per Serving: Calories 387; Fat 9. 36g; Sodium 484mg; Carbs 55. 74g; Fiber 7. 6g; Sugar 23. 06g; Protein 20. 64g

Quinoa, Oats and Apple Casserole

Prep time: 10 minutes | **Cook time:** 7 hours | **Serves:** 6

1 cup gluten-free steel-cut oats

½ cup quinoa, rinsed

4½ cups unsweetened vanilla almond milk (or water), plus more for serving

4 Medjool dates, chopped

1 apple peeled and diced

2 teaspoons cinnamon

¼ teaspoon nutmeg

1 teaspoon vanilla extract

¼ cup crushed walnuts (optional)

1. Spray the inside of the pot with nonstick spray. 2. Combine the steel-cut oats, quinoa, dates, apple, almond milk, nutmeg, cinnamon, and vanilla in the pot. 3. Cover, turn dial to Slow Cook and cook on high for 2 hours, or on low for 6 to 7 hours. 4. Stir well before serving. Top each serving with walnuts and a splash of almond milk if you desired.

Per Serving: Calories 246; Fat 6. 13g; Sodium 115mg; Carbs 48. 8g; Fiber 6. 6g; Sugar 25. 46g; Protein 6. 38g

Chapter 2 Vegetable and Sides Recipes

Potato Cheese Tacos

Prep time: 10 minutes | **Cook time:** 8½-9½ hours | **Serves:** 4

4 russet potatoes, cubed	1 (12-ounce) can evaporated milk
1 onion, chopped	2 tablespoons cornstarch
3 cloves garlic, minced	1 (4-ounce) can chopped green chile, drained
2 tablespoons olive oil	4 taco shells
½ teaspoon salt	1 cup shredded pepper jack cheese
⅛ teaspoon pepper	½ cup chopped tomato
½ cup water	

1. Combine potatoes, oil, onion, garlic, salt, and pepper in the pot, mix well. Pour water over; cover with the lid and turn dial to Slow Cook, cook on low for 8–9 hours or until potatoes are tender. 2. In small bowl, mix together the milk and cornstarch. Stir into potato mixture along with chiles. Cover with the lid and cook on Slow Cook function at high heat for 20–30 minutes or until mixture is thickened. 3. Heat taco shells in the oven according to package directions until crisp, about 6–7 minutes. Make tacos with potato mixture, cheese, and tomatoes.

Per Serving: Calories 614; Fat 21. 79g; Sodium 644mg; Carbs 88. 11g; Fiber 6. 9g; Sugar 9g; Protein 19. 45g

Eggplant Parmesan with Almonds

Prep time: 10 minutes | **Cook time:** 8-9 hours | **Serves:** 8

5 large eggplants, peeled and sliced ½-inch thick	2 tablespoons olive oil
2 onions, chopped	1 teaspoon dried Italian seasoning
6 garlic cloves, minced	½ cup grated Parmesan cheese
2 (8-ounce) BPA-free cans low-sodium tomato sauce	½ cup chopped toasted almonds

1. Layer the eggplant slices with the onions and garlic in the pot. 2. Combine the tomato sauce, olive oil, and Italian seasoning in a bowl. Pour the tomato sauce mixture into the pot. 3. Cover with the lid and turn dial to Slow Cook, cook on low for 8 to 9 hours, or until the eggplant is tender. 4. Mix the Parmesan cheese and almonds in a small bowl. Sprinkle over the eggplant mixture and serve.

Per Serving: Calories 187; Fat 5. 89g; Sodium 527mg; Carbs 30. 16g; Fiber 12. 5g; Sugar 16. 31g; Protein 6. 32g

Vegetarian Curry with Wild Rice

Prep time: 10 minutes | Cook time: 8-9 hours | Serves: 4

1 tablespoon olive oil	½ cup dark raisins
1 onion, chopped	¼ cup dried currants
2 cloves garlic, minced	½ teaspoon salt
1 tablespoon minced gingerroot	⅛ teaspoon pepper
2 teaspoons curry powder	1 (15-ounce) can chickpeas, drained
1 cup wild rice	2 cups vegetable broth
1 pear, peeled, cored, and chopped	½ cup apple chutney
1 apple, peeled and chopped	

1. Add olive oil to the pot. Turn dial to Sear/Sauté, set temperature to LO, and press START/STOP to begin cooking. Once the oil is heated, add onions, gingerroot, garlic, and curry powder; cook and stir for 5 minutes. Add salt, pepper, chickpeas, Broth, and Chutney to the pot, bring to a simmer. Press START/STOP to turn off the Sear/Sauté function. Transfer the mixture to a bowl. 2. Place wild rice in bottom of the pot. Spread the pears, apples, raisins, and currants on top. 3. Pour the chickpeas mixture into the pot. 4. Cover with the lid and turn dial to Slow COOK, cook on low for 8–9 hours or until wild rice is tender. Stir gently to mix.

Per Serving: Calories 384; Fat 6. 94g; Sodium 736mg; Carbs 71. 51g; Fiber 12. 1g; Sugar 17. 63g; Protein 13. 49g

Spiced Cauliflower, Potatoes, & Peas

Prep time: 10 minutes | Cook time: 3 hours | Serves: 4

Cooking spray	1 teaspoon ground cumin
1 head cauliflower, rinsed and cut into 1" chunks	2 teaspoons chili powder
1 large potato, peeled and diced	1 tablespoon garam masala
1 medium onion, peeled and diced	2 teaspoons kosher salt
½ cup frozen peas, completely defrosted	½ teaspoon turmeric powder
1 teaspoon ground ginger	1 tablespoon vegetable oil
3 cloves garlic, minced	¼ cup packed fresh cilantro leaves

1. Spray the inside of the pot with cooking spray. 2. Add all the ingredients except cilantro to the pot, stir well. 3. Cover with the lid and turn dial to Slow Cook, cook on low for 3 hours. Transfer to serving dish and top with the cilantro leaves.

Per Serving: Calories 150; Fat 4. 14g; Sodium 1234mg; Carbs 25. 92g; Fiber 5. 2g; Sugar 3. 4g; Protein 4. 58g

Juicy Cranberry–Walnut and Green Beans

Prep time: 10 minutes | **Cook time:** 5-7 hours | **Serves:** 8

2 pounds fresh green beans	½ teaspoon salt
1 onion, chopped	⅛ teaspoon freshly ground black pepper
1 cup dried cranberries	1 cup coarsely chopped toasted walnuts
⅓ cup orange juice	

1. Mix together the green beans, cranberries, onion, orange juice, salt, and pepper in the pot. Cover with the lid and turn dial to Slow Cook, cook on low for 5 to 7 hours, or until the green beans are tender. 2. Add the walnuts and serve.

Per Serving: Calories 118; Fat 7. 1g; Sodium 149mg; Carbs 13. 04g; Fiber 3. 1g; Sugar 6. 34g; Protein 3. 02g

Cheesy Summer Vegetables Lasagna

Prep time: 15 minutes | **Cook time:** 4-5 hours | **Serves:** 5

1 tablespoon butter	1 teaspoon dried Italian seasoning
1 tablespoon olive oil	½ teaspoon salt
½ eggplant, peeled and cubed	¼ teaspoon pepper
1 yellow summer squash, peeled and cubed	1 cup part-skim ricotta cheese
1 (8-ounce) package sliced fresh mushrooms	1 egg
1 onion, chopped	½ (8-ounce) package cream cheese
2 cloves garlic, minced	1 cup shredded mozzarella cheese
1 (6-ounce) can tomato paste	¼ cup grated Parmesan cheese, divided
2 cup vegetable broth	6 lasagna noodles

1. Add butter and olive oil to the pot. Turn dial to Sear/Sauté, set temperature to LO, and press SART/ STOP to begin cooking. Once the butter is melted, add eggplant, cook and stir until crisp-tender, about 5 minutes. Transfer to large bowl. Add squash and mushrooms to the pot; cook and stir until crisp-tender, about 5 minutes. Transfer to the same large bowl with slotted spoon. 2. Add onion and garlic to the pot; cook and stir for 5 minutes. Stir in tomato paste, Broth, salt, seasoning, and pepper; bring to a simmer. Transfer to a bowl. 3. In a separate large bowl, combine ricotta cheese, egg, and cream cheese; beat until blended. Stir in mozzarella cheese and 2 tablespoons Parmesan cheese. 4. Spray the pot with nonstick cooking spray. Add a spoonful of the tomato sauce to the bottom. Top with 2 lasagna noodles, then a layer of the squash mixture. Top with ricotta mixture. Repeat layers, ending with ricotta mixture. Pour the broth mixture into the pot. 5. Sprinkle with remaining 2 tablespoons Parmesan cheese. Cover with the lid and turn dial to Slow Cook, cook on high for 4–5 hours or until lasagna noodles are tender. Press START/ STOP to turn off the Slow Cook function, remove cover, and let stand for 15 minutes before serving.

Per Serving: Calories 461; Fat 26. 47g; Sodium 1104mg; Carbs 34g; Fiber 5. 8g; Sugar 12. 37g; Protein 25. 18g

Acorn Squash & Chickpea Stew over Couscous

Prep time: 10 minutes | **Cook time:** 9-10 hours | **Serves:** 4

1 acorn squash, peeled and cubed	½ teaspoon dried oregano leaves
1 onion, chopped	⅛ teaspoon pepper
2 cloves garlic, minced	1 (15-ounce) can chickpeas, drained
2 carrots, sliced	½ cup golden raisins
3 cups vegetable broth	1½ cups couscous
4 cups water	⅓ cup crumbled feta cheese
½ teaspoon salt	

1. Combine all ingredients except couscous, 1 cup broth, 2 cups water, and feta in the pot. Cover with the lid and turn dial to Slow Cook, cook on low for 9–10 hours or until vegetables are very tender. 2. In a large saucepan, heat 1 cup of broth and 2 cups of water until boiling. Add couscous, cover and remove from heat. After 5 minutes, use a fork to fluff the couscous and transfer it to a serving bowl. 3. Stir mixture in the pot and spoon over couscous. Sprinkle with feta cheese and serve.

Per Serving: Calories 307; Fat 4. 73g; Sodium 576mg; Carbs 59. 49g; Fiber 7. 9g; Sugar 16. 64g; Protein 10. 46g

Creamy Cheesy Potatoes Casserole

Prep time: 10 minutes | **Cook time:** 8-9 hours | **Serves:** 8

1 20-ounce package frozen hash brown potatoes, thawed	1 (3-ounce) package cream cheese, cubed
1 sweet potato, peeled	¾ cup sour cream
1 tablespoon butter	¾ cup shredded Swiss cheese
1 onion, chopped	½ cup milk
3 cloves garlic, minced	1 teaspoon dried basil leaves
1 (10-ounce) jar Alfredo sauce	⅛ teaspoon pepper

1. Drain the hash brown potatoes and place in the pot. Coarsely grate the sweet potatoes and add to the pot; mix gently. 2. In a large skillet, melt some butter over medium heat. Then, cook and stir onions and garlic until they become soft, which usually takes around 6 to 7 minutes. After that, transfer the mixture to the pot and mix well. 3. Add Alfredo sauce, cream cheese, sour cream, milk, Swiss cheese, basil, and pepper to skillet; cook and stir over medium-low heat until cream cheese melts. Pour over potatoes in the pot. 4. Cover with the lid and turn dial to Slow Cook, cook on low for 8–9 hours or until potatoes are tender and mixture is bubbling. Serve warm.

Per Serving: Calories 400; Fat 23. 84g; Sodium 1255mg; Carbs 34g; Fiber 2. 9g; Sugar 4. 76g; Protein 12. 75g

Spicy Corn Bread

Prep time: 10 minutes | Cook time: 2-3 hours | Serves: 6

2 (8-ounce) packages corn muffin mix	1 cup frozen corn
1 tablespoon chili powder, divided	1 (4-ounce) can chopped green chiles, drained
2 eggs, beaten	¾ cup shredded Colby cheese
⅓ cup milk	⅓ cup mild salsa
⅓ cup sour cream	

1. Combine both packages of muffin mix and 2 teaspoons of chili powder in a large bowl, and mix them. 2. In a medium bowl, mix eggs, milk, and sour cream well, then add them to the muffin mix and stir until they are combined. 3. Next, add corn and stir. In a small bowl, mix drained chiles, cheese, and salsa. 4. Spray the pot with nonstick cooking spray, then spoon half of the muffin mix batter into the pot. Add the green chile mixture on top, and then add the remaining batter. Smooth the top and sprinkle with the remaining 1 teaspoon of chili powder. 5. Cover with the lid and turn dial to Slow Cook, cook on high for 2–3 hours, or until top springs back when lightly touched. Press START/STOP to turn off the Slow Cook function, uncover, then top with foil, leaving a corner vented, and cool for 20 minutes. 6. Serve by scooping out hot bread with a large spoon.

Per Serving: Calories 296; Fat 14. 75g; Sodium 645mg; Carbs 29. 04g; Fiber 2. 6g; Sugar 2. 46g; Protein 12. 09g

Honey–Mustard Glazed Carrots

Prep time: 10 minutes | Cook time: 7-8 hours | Serves: 8

8 carrots, sliced	⅓ cup apricot preserves
1 cup orange juice	3 tablespoons Dijon mustard
2 tablespoons butter	¼ teaspoon salt
¼ cup honey	⅛ teaspoon white pepper
2 tablespoons brown sugar	

1. Combine carrots and orange juice in the pot. Cover with the lid and turn dial to Slow Cook, cook on low for 7-8 hours or until carrots are tender. Drain, reserving ¼ cup of the liquid. 2. In a small saucepan, mix the rest of the ingredients and heat them over medium heat while stirring, until the sugar has dissolved. Pour over carrots in the pot. 3. Cover and cook on high for 30-40 minutes more until carrots are glazed.

Per Serving: Calories 98; Fat 3. 15g; Sodium 164mg; Carbs 18. 34g; Fiber 0. 8g; Sugar 16. 31g; Protein 0. 71g

Cauliflower Curry with Peas

Prep time: 10 minutes | **Cook time:** 4-6 hours | **Serves:** 4

Cooking spray
Florets from 1 head of cauliflower (about 2 cups), rinsed and drained
1 (15-ounce) can diced tomatoes, drained
1 medium onion, peeled and diced
1 large baking potato, peeled and cut into 1" cubes
1 cup low-fat coconut milk

1½ teaspoons curry powder
½ teaspoon ground coriander
½ teaspoon ground cinnamon
¼ teaspoon black pepper
⅛ teaspoon crushed red pepper
1 teaspoon kosher salt
1 cup frozen peas, defrosted

1. Spray the pot with cooking spray. 2. Add cauliflower, tomatoes, onion, and potato to the pot. 3. Mix together the remaining ingredients except the peas in a bowl and pour over vegetables into the pot. 4. Cover with the lid and turn dial to Slow Cook, cook on low for 4–6 hours or until the cauliflower is tender. 5. Uncover and stir in peas. Re-cover and cook on low heat setting for 10–15 minutes or until peas are heated through.

Per Serving: Calories 167; Fat 2. 97g; Sodium 956mg; Carbs 30. 62g; Fiber 7. 2g; Sugar 8. 08g; Protein 6. 96g

Healthy Quinoa Tacos

Prep time: 10 minutes | **Cook time:** 10 hours | **Serves:** 4

1½ cups quinoa
6 cups vegetable stock
2 tablespoons chopped chipotles in adobo, or more as desired

Toppings:
Baby spinach leaves
Chopped tomatoes
Chopped onions
Chopped fresh cilantro
Chopped jalapeños

1 teaspoon smoked paprika
1 tablespoon taco seasoning mix
Whole-wheat tortillas

Chopped lettuce
Grated cheese
Queso fresco
Salsa

1. In the pot, combine all the taco ingredients except the tortillas and the toppings. 2. Cover with the lid and turn dial to Slow Cook, cook on low for 10 hours or on high for 5 hours. 3. Warm the tortillas in a dry skillet over medium heat. Fill the warm tortillas with the filling and top with your favorite ingredients. Fold in half to serve.

Per Serving: Calories 530; Fat 13. 85g; Sodium 1265mg; Carbs 74. 42g; Fiber 11. 5g; Sugar 8. 84g; Protein 28. 51g

Lemony Rosemary Fingerling Potatoes

Prep time: 10 minutes | Cook time: 3-4 hours | Serves: 6

2 tablespoons olive oil	¼ teaspoon black pepper
1½ pounds fingerling potatoes, cut into small cubes	2 tablespoons fresh rosemary, chopped
1 teaspoon salt	1 tablespoon fresh lemon juice

1. Add the olive oil, potatoes, salt, and pepper to the pot. Cover with the lid and turn dial to Slow Cook, cook on low heat for 3–4 hours or on high for 1½–2 hours. Potatoes are done when they can be easily pierced with a fork. 2. When cooking is complete, remove the cover and mix in the rosemary and lemon juice.

Per Serving: Calories 129; Fat 4. 65g; Sodium 395mg; Carbs 20. 18g; Fiber 2. 6g; Sugar 0. 95g; Protein 2. 33g

Orange–Soy Kale and Mushroom Salad

Prep time: 10 minutes | Cook time: 10 minutes | Serves: 2

For the Dressing:	
½ teaspoon orange zest	1 small shallot, minced
1 tablespoon freshly squeezed orange juice	2 tablespoons extra-virgin olive oil
1 teaspoon low-sodium soy sauce	Freshly ground black pepper
For the Salad:	
1 cup quartered cremini mushrooms	1 bunch Lacinato kale, ribs removed

To make the dressing: 1. Mix together the orange zest and juice, soy sauce, and shallots in a glass jar. Stir them well. 2. While whisking constantly, slowly add the olive oil to the mixture to create an emulsified dressing. 3. Finally, season the dressing with a few twists of black pepper.

To make the salad: 1. Add the mushrooms to the pot. Pour the dressing over them, allowing them to soften slightly while you prepare the kale. 2. Cut the kale into very thin ribbons and transfer to the pot, stir well. Cover and turn dial to Sear/Sauté, set temperature to LO, and press START/STOP to begin cooking. Allow ingredients to cook for 10 minutes. 3. Serve warm.

Per Serving: Calories 78; Fat 6. 27g; Sodium 207mg; Carbs 4. 38g; Fiber 1g; Sugar 2. 29g; Protein 2. 29g

Rice and Apple Stuffed Acorn Squash

Prep time: 10 minutes | **Cook time:** 6-8 hours | **Serves:** 2

1 cup cooked brown rice	vegan), divided
1 small apple, cored and diced	1 acorn squash, halved and seeded
2 tablespoons dried cranberries	2 tablespoons honey (or maple syrup if vegan)
2 tablespoons chopped nuts (pecans, almonds, walnuts)	1 teaspoon ground cinnamon
2 teaspoons unsalted butter (or extra-virgin olive oil if	¼ teaspoon ground nutmeg

1. Combine rice, apple, cranberries, and nuts in a big bowl. 2. Place 1 teaspoon of butter in each squash half and stuff them with the rice mixture. 3. Pour 1 cup of water into the pot. Place the stuffed squash in the bottom of the pot, stuffed-side up. 4. In a small bowl, combine the cinnamon, honey, and nutmeg. Sprinkle over the squash and filling. 5. Cover, turn dial to Slow Cook. Cook on low for 6 to 8 hours, or until the squash is tender, and serve.

Per Serving: Calories 384; Fat 9. 05g; Sodium 38mg; Carbs 77. 2g; Fiber 8. 2g; Sugar 27. 51g; Protein 5. 1g

Beans and Corns Enchilada Casserole

Prep time: 10 minutes | **Cook time:** 8 hours | **Serves:** 6

Cooking spray	1 cup chopped onion
2 cups Poblano Mole, ½ cup reserved	12 corn tortillas
3 cups cooked beans (black, pinto, red, or a mixture)	2 cups grated queso quesadilla or Monterey Jack
2 cups fresh or frozen corn	cheese, ½ cup reserved
1 cup diced sweet potato or winter squash	½ cup chopped fresh cilantro

1. Spray the pot with cooking spray. 2. Mix the beans, sweet potato, corn, onion, and 1. 5 cups of mole sauce in a big bowl. Spread a small amount of this mixture at the bottom of a pot. 3. Place a layer of tortillas on top of it. Add a layer of vegetable mixture on the tortillas and sprinkle some cheese and cilantro on top. Repeat these layers until all the filling is used, and end it with a layer of tortillas. 4. Spread the reserved ½ cup of mole on the tortillas and sprinkle with the reserved ½ cup of cheese. 5. Cover with the lid and turn dial to Slow Cook, cook on low for 8 hours or on high for 4 hours, and serve hot.

Per Serving: Calories 577; Fat 24. 92g; Sodium 645mg; Carbs 67. 09g; Fiber 14. 4g; Sugar 8. 92g; Protein 25. 81g

Sweet Potato Hash with Nuts

Prep time: 10 minutes | **Cook time:** 2-4 hours | **Serves:** 6

4 pounds sweet potatoes, peeled and chopped	½ teaspoon salt
1 cup water	1 tablespoon unsalted butter
¼ cup honey or maple syrup	½ cup coarsely chopped pecans or walnuts, lightly
2 teaspoons ground cinnamon	toasted
¼ teaspoon ground nutmeg	

1. In the pot, mix together the potatoes, water, nutmeg, salt, honey, cinnamon, and butter. 2. Cover with the lid and turn dial to Slow Cook, cook on low for 2 to 4 hours, or until the potatoes are soft. 3. Using an immersion blender, potato masher, or the back of a large spoon, mash the sweet potatoes until they reach your desired consistency. 4. Top with the chopped nuts and serve.

Per Serving: Calories 325; Fat 5. 96g; Sodium 215mg; Carbs 63. 3g; Fiber 7. 6g; Sugar 10. 49g; Protein 7. 25g

Sweet & Sour Pulled Jackfruit

Prep time: 10 minutes | **Cook time:** 6-8 hours | **Serves:** 8

4 (20-ounce) cans jackfruit, drained and rinsed	¼ cup apple cider vinegar
2 cups ketchup	¼ cup maple syrup
1 cup water	1 tablespoon powdered mustard
1 small onion, diced	1 teaspoon salt
2 celery stalks, diced	½ teaspoon freshly ground black pepper
¼ cup extra-virgin olive oil	1½ teaspoons gluten-free Worcestershire sauce
¼ cup freshly squeezed lemon juice	

1. Add the jackfruit, ketchup, olive oil, water, onion, lemon juice, vinegar, maple syrup, celery, mustard, salt, pepper, and Worcestershire sauce to the pot. Stir to mix well. 2. Cover, turn dial to Slow Cook and cook on low for 6 to 8 hours. 3. Transfer the jackfruit to a plate. Using two forks, twist to pull the jackfruit into shreds. Return it to the pot and heat through before serving.

Per Serving: Calories 533; Fat 3. 7g; Sodium 976mg; Carbs 132. 1g; Fiber 4. 5g; Sugar 20. 14g; Protein 2. 51g

Cheese Tofu and Mushroom Enchiladas

Prep time: 10 minutes | **Cook time:** 8 hours | **Serves:** 6

12 ounces firm tofu, drained, pressed, and cut into bite-size cubes	½ teaspoon sea salt
2 tablespoons taco seasoning mix	½ cup chopped fresh cilantro
2 poblano chiles, fire-roasted, peeled, seeded, and chopped	½ cup Mexican crema or sour cream
1 pound portabello mushrooms, chopped	1½ cups grated queso quesadilla or pepper Jack cheese, divided
½ medium onion, chopped	Cooking spray
1 teaspoon ground cumin	12 corn tortillas
	1 cup Green Salsa

The night before: 1. Mix the tofu and taco seasoning thoroughly in a big bowl, making sure that the tofu is coated on all sides. Add more seasoning if necessary. 2. After that, cover the bowl and keep it in the refrigerator overnight.

In the morning: 1. Add the poblano, onion, mushrooms, cumin, salt, and cilantro to the large bowl with the tofu. Gently stir in the crema and ½ cup of the cheese. 2. Spray the pot with cooking spray. 3. Heat the tortillas in a dry skillet on medium heat. Put some of the filling on a tortilla, roll it up, and place it in the pot with the seam facing down. Repeat this process with the remaining filling and tortillas. 4. Cover the enchiladas with the green salsa and top with the remaining 1 cup of cheese. Cover with the lid and turn dial to Slow Cook, cook on low for 8 hours. Serve hot.

Per Serving: Calories 571; Fat 18. 31g; Sodium 955mg; Carbs 88. 15g; Fiber 13. 6g; Sugar 5. 79g; Protein 26. 29g

Juicy Beets

Prep time: 10 minutes | **Cook time:** 4 hours | **Serves:** 4

12 baby beets, halved, ends trimmed	¼ red onion, sliced
1 cup orange juice	½ teaspoon pepper
Juice of ½ lime	

Add all ingredients to the pot. Cover with the lid and turn dial to Slow Cook, cook on low for 4 hours.

Per Serving: Calories 140; Fat 0. 51g; Sodium 194mg; Carbs 31. 75g; Fiber 7. 2g; Sugar 22. 21g; Protein 4. 53g

Spicy No–Cheese Enchilada Casserole

Prep time: 10 minutes | **Cook time:** 6 hours | **Serves:** 6

2 zucchinis, diced
1 medium onion, chopped
1½ medium jalapeños, seeded and chopped, or more as desired
2 cups fresh or frozen corn
2 pounds tempeh, chopped
½ cup chopped fresh cilantro

1 teaspoon ground cumin
1 teaspoon ancho chili powder
½ teaspoon garlic powder
½ cup sliced black olives
8 Roma tomatoes, chopped, or 1 (28-ounce) can diced fire-roasted tomatoes
6 blue corn or other corn tortillas

1. Spray the pot with cooking spray. 2. Mix everything together, except for the tortillas, in a big bowl. Spread a small amount of the vegetable mix on the bottom of the pot, and then put a layer of tortillas on top. 3. Spoon a thicker layer of the vegetable mixture on the tortillas. Cover with another layer of tortillas and repeat until the ingredients are used up, ending with a layer of tortillas. 4. Cover and turn dial to Slow Cook, cook on low for 6 hours or on high for 3½ hours. 5. Once done, cut into slices and serve hot.

Per Serving: Calories 615; Fat 24. 3g; Sodium 520mg; Carbs 63. 41g; Fiber 4. 2g; Sugar 5. 1g; Protein 41. 83g

Chapter 3 Snack and Appetizer Recipes

Candied Almonds

Prep time: 10 minutes | Cook time: 2 hours | Serves: 25

1 lb. whole unsalted almonds	½ tsp sea salt
1½ cups granulated sugar	2 egg whites
2 tsp cinnamon	¼ tsp vanilla extract

1. In a bowl, combine the sugar, cinnamon and salt with nuts, mix well and set aside. 2. In another bowl, whisk the egg whites with vanilla extract until frothy. 3. Bring the nuts to the egg mixture and coat all the nuts. 4. Put the nut mixture into the pot that has been sprayed with cooking spray. 5. Cover with the lid and turn dial to Slow Cook, cook on low for 2 hours, stirring every 30 minutes. 6. When done cooking, spread nuts on a baking sheet, lined with parchment paper, to cool.

Per Serving: Calories 135; Fat 10. 02g; Sodium 51mg; Carbs 9. 39g; Fiber 2g; Sugar 6. 72g; Protein 4. 15g

Yummy Oriental Snack Mix

Prep time: 10 minutes | Cook time: 55 minutes | Serves: 28

6 tbsp butter or margarine	4 cups Bugles original corn snacks
1 tsp garlic powder	2 cups chow Mein noodles
2 tbsp soy sauce	1 cup pretzel sticks
1 package (1 oz.) Chow Mein oriental mix	1 cup salted peanuts
4 cups Corn Chex cereal	1 cup wasabi peas

1. Melt butter in a small saucepan over medium heat, and then remove from heat. Mix the Chow Mein seasoning mix, garlic powder, and soy sauce until it's well combined. 2. In the pot, mix all the other ingredients except for the wasabi peas. Pour the melted butter mixture over the cereal mixture and toss everything together evenly to coat it. 3. Turn the dial to Bake and set the temperature to 250°F, bake for 50 to 55 minutes, stirring every 15 minutes, until mixture looks dry and crisp. 4. Pour mixture onto paper towels. Cool 15 minutes. Stir in wasabi peas before serving. Store in a tightly covered container.

Per Serving: Calories 225; Fat 9. 39g; Sodium 187mg; Carbs 31. 33g; Fiber 3. 4g; Sugar 1. 94g; Protein 5. 83g

Lemony Hummus

Prep time: 10 minutes | **Cook time:** 8 hours | **Serves:** 20

1 pound dried chickpeas, rinsed and drained	2 teaspoons lemon zest
Water, as needed	3 cloves garlic
3 tablespoons tahini	½ teaspoon kosher salt, or to taste
4 tablespoons lemon juice	¼ teaspoon white pepper, or to taste

1. In the pot, add the chickpeas and cover with water by several inches. Soak overnight. 2. The next day, drain the chickpeas and replace the water. Cover and select the Slow Cook function, cook on low for 8 hours. Drain, reserving the liquid. 3. Put the cooked chickpeas, tahini, lemon juice, lemon zest, garlic, salt, and pepper into a food processor. 4. Blend until it becomes smooth, and add the reserved liquid as required to get the desired consistency. 5. Taste it and add more salt and pepper if necessary.

Per Serving: Calories 101; Fat 2. 59g; Sodium 67mg; Carbs 15. 17g; Fiber 3g; Sugar 2. 53g; Protein 5. 07g

Rice and Meat Stuffed Grape Leaves

Prep time: 10 minutes | **Cook time:** 4-6 hours | **Serves:** 30

1 (16-ounce) jar grape leaves (about 60 leaves)	2 tablespoons minced parsley
Cooking spray, as needed	1 tablespoon dried mint
¾ pound ground beef, chicken, or veal	1 tablespoon ground fennel
1 shallot, minced	¼ teaspoon freshly ground black pepper
¾ cup cooked brown or white rice	⅛ teaspoon salt
¼ cup minced dill	2 cups water
½ cup lemon juice, divided use	

1. Firstly, follow the instructions on the grape leaf package and keep them aside. Then, use a nonstick skillet sprayed with cooking spray to cook the meat and shallot until the meat is fully cooked. 2. Remove any extra fat and put it in a large bowl. Add rice, dill, ¼ cup of lemon juice, parsley, mint, fennel, pepper, and salt to the bowl and mix all ingredients well. 3. Place a grape leaf, stem side up, with the top of the leaf pointing away from you on a clean work surface. 4. Place 1 teaspoon filling in the middle of the leaf. Fold the bottom toward the middle and then fold in the sides. Roll it toward the top to seal. Repeat with the other leaves. 5. Place the rolled grape leaves in the pot. Pour in the water and remaining lemon juice. 6. Cover with the lid and select the Slow Cook function, cook on low for 4–6 hours. Serve warm or cold.

Per Serving: Calories 41; Fat 2. 51g; Sodium 19mg; Carbs 2. 13g; Fiber 0. 9g; Sugar 0. 22g; Protein 3. 39g

Crispy Coconut Chicken Fingers

Prep time: 10 minutes | **Cook time:** 2-4 hours | **Serves:** 8

Cooking spray
3 tablespoons fresh lemon juice
3 tablespoons fresh lime juice
3 tablespoons spicy brown mustard
½ cup plain toasted bread crumbs
½ cup unsweetened shredded coconut
½ teaspoon kosher salt

¼ teaspoon ground black pepper
¼ teaspoon curry powder
¼ teaspoon dried oregano
4 skinless, boneless chicken breasts, cut into 2" × 1" inch strips
¼ cup (½ stick) margarine, melted
½ cup honey-mustard dipping sauce

1. Spray the inside of the pot with the cooking spray. Set aside. 2. Mix the lemon juice, lime juice, and mustard in a small bowl. In a separate bowl, combine bread crumbs, coconut, salt, pepper, curry powder, and oregano. 3. Dip chicken strips in the mustard mixture and then in the bread crumb mixture. Place the coated chicken in a prepared pot and pour melted margarine on top. 4. Cover and select the Slow Cook function, cook on high for 2–4 hours, or until the chicken fingers are fully cooked. 5. Serve with honey-mustard dipping sauce if desired.

Per Serving: Calories 162; Fat 12. 56g; Sodium 371mg; Carbs 10. 38g; Fiber 0. 9g; Sugar 3. 56g; Protein 2. 51g

Bell Pepper & Olive Salad with Maple–Mustard Dressing

Prep time: 10 minutes | **Cook time:** 3 hours | **Serves:** 4

For the Salad:
2 medium red bell peppers, quartered
2 hearts romaine lettuce
For the Dressing:
4 tablespoons red wine vinegar
2 tablespoons Dijon mustard
1 tablespoon maple syrup

½ pint grape or cherry tomatoes
1 (5. 6-ounce) jar green olives, drained

1 teaspoon lemon juice
¾ teaspoon Italian seasoning

1. Make the salad: Place the bell peppers in the pot. Cover with the lid and select the Slow Cook function, cook on Low for 2½ to 3 hours. Carefully remove the peppers. When they are cool enough to handle, peel off the skins and discard. Use a paring knife to get them started (although the skins will likely be falling off). Slice the peppers into ½-inch-wide strips. 2. After letting the peppers cool, dice the romaine and put it in a big bowl. Halve the tomatoes and add them to the bowl, along with the olives and the cooked and peeled peppers. 3. Create the dressing by combining vinegar, mustard, maple syrup, lemon juice, and Italian seasoning in a small jar with a lid. Shake the jar thoroughly to mix the dressing well. 4. Pour the dressing over the salad and mix well before serving.

Per Serving: Calories 45; Fat 0. 59g; Sodium 139mg; Carbs 8. 48g; Fiber 2g; Sugar 5. 98g; Protein 1. 11g

SavoryVeggie Pot Stuffing

Prep time: 10 minutes | **Cook time:** 3-4 hours | **Serves:** 6

Nonstick cooking spray (optional)
2 (12-ounce) packages stuffing cubes (about 12 cups)
2 small or 1 large onion, diced (about 2 cups)
6 large celery stalks, diced (about 2 cups)
1 (8-ounce) package white button mushrooms, diced
2 teaspoons dried sage
1 teaspoon poultry seasoning
1 teaspoon marjoram
1 teaspoon crushed or ground fennel seed
⅓ cup chopped fresh parsley
Ground black pepper
Salt (optional)
3½ to 5 cups low-sodium vegetable broth or store-bought, divided

1. Coat the inside of the pot with cooking spray. 2. Add the onions, celery, and mushrooms to the pot. 3. Turn dial to Sear/Sauté, set temperature to HI, and press START/STOP to begin cooking. Allow ingredients to cook for 5 to 7 minutes, or until the onions are translucent, adding a splash of water or broth to avoid sticking. 4. Stir in the sage, stuffing cubes, fennel seed, poultry seasoning, marjoram, parsley, pepper, and salt (if using) and cook for another minute or so. Press START/STOP to turn off the Sear/Sauté function. 5. Add 3½ cups of broth, stirring to combine. Add more broth, ½ cup at a time, to achieve your desired consistency. 6. Cover with the lid and turn dial to Slow Cook, cook on High for 45 minutes, then turn the heat to Low and cook for 3 to 4 hours, until the stuffing reaches the consistency you prefer. 7. Add more broth as needed during the cooking time for a moister stuffing.
Per Serving: Calories 258; Fat 12. 76g; Sodium 221mg; Carbs 35. 28g; Fiber 7. 1g; Sugar 22. 79g; Protein 4. 17g

Spicy Red Beans and Rice Casserole

Prep time: 10 minutes | **Cook time:** 3-5 hours | **Serves:** 4

1 medium green bell pepper, diced
1 medium onion, diced
2 celery stalks, diced
4 garlic cloves, minced
1 (14. 5-ounce) can light or dark red kidney beans, drained and rinsed
1½ cups brown rice
4 to 6 chipotle peppers in adobo sauce or store-bought,
finely chopped
3 cups low-sodium vegetable broth or store-bought
2 teaspoons smoked paprika
1 teaspoon ground cumin
1 teaspoon chili powder
½ teaspoon cayenne powder
Ground black pepper
Salt (optional)

1. Put the bell pepper, garlic, beans, onion, celery, and rice in the pot. Add the chipotle peppers, scraping the sauce from the cutting board into the cooker. Add the broth, paprika, cumin, chili powder, and cayenne. Season with black pepper and salt (if using). 2. Cover with the lid and turn the dial to Slow Cook, cook on High for 2 hours or on Low for 3 to 5 hours, until the liquid is absorbed and the rice is tender. 3. Store leftovers in the refrigerator for up to 4 days.
Per Serving: Calories 422; Fat 3. 65g; Sodium 453mg; Carbs 85. 56g; Fiber 11. 4g; Sugar 10. 23g; Protein 14. 71g

Gingered Rice and Veggie Pilaf with Apricot

Prep time: 10 minutes | **Cook time:** 5-6 hours | **Serves:** 4

1 small onion, diced	6 cups low-sodium vegetable broth or store-bought
2 celery stalks, diced	1 tablespoon low-sodium soy sauce, tamari, or coconut
2 carrots, diced	aminos
1 cup wild rice	4 ounces of shiitake mushrooms, stemmed
2 cups brown rice	1 cup chopped pecans
1 (1-inch) piece fresh ginger, peeled and minced, or 1	½ cup chopped dried apricots
teaspoon ground ginger	½ bunch flat-leaf parsley, coarsely chopped
1 teaspoon garlic powder	

1. Put the onion, celery, and carrots in the pot. Add the wild rice, brown rice garlic powder, ginger, broth, and soy sauce. 2. Slice the mushroom caps into strips and add to the pot. Stir to combine. Cover with the lid and turn the dial to Slow Cook, cook on High for 3 hours or on Low for 5 to 6 hours, until all of the liquid is absorbed. 3. Fluff with a fork and top with the pecans, apricots, and parsley to serve.

Per Serving: Calories 812; Fat 22. 49g; Sodium 380mg; Carbs 140. 74g; Fiber 13. 4g; Sugar 25. 68g; Protein 21. 18g

Hoisin–Honey Glazed Chicken Wings

Prep time: 10 minutes | **Cook time:** 4 hours | **Serves:** 8

3 pounds chicken wings, tips cut off	½ cup soy sauce
1 teaspoon paprika	½ cup hoisin sauce
½ teaspoon sea salt	¼ cup rice wine
½ teaspoon freshly ground black pepper	2 garlic cloves, minced
1 cup honey	1 teaspoon minced fresh ginger

1. Put the wings in the pot and sprinkle paprika, salt, and pepper on them. 2. Combine honey, soy sauce, hoisin sauce, rice wine, garlic, and ginger in a medium bowl by whisking them together. 3. Pour the mixture of honey over the wings in the pot and stir well to cover them. 4. Cover with the lid and turn the dial to Slow Cook, cook on low for 4 hours, or until the wings register 165°F on a food thermometer. 5. Preheat the broiler. Take the wings out of the sauce and put them on a broiler pan in a single layer. 6. Use some of the sauce from the pot to brush the wings. 7. Broil the wings for 3 to 4 minutes until they become crispy. 8. Turn the wings over, brush them with more sauce, and broil for another 3 to 4 minutes. 9. Serve the wings hot.

Per Serving: Calories 439; Fat 10. 26g; Sodium 785mg; Carbs 48. 31g; Fiber 1. 8g; Sugar 42. 31g; Protein 39. 76g

Cheese–Beer Fondue

Prep time: 10 minutes | **Cook time:** 2 hours | **Serves:** 8

2 cups shredded Swiss cheese	¼ teaspoon freshly grated nutmeg
2 cups shredded sharp Cheddar cheese	2 tablespoons all-purpose flour
1 garlic clove, minced	1 cup light beer
½ teaspoon dry mustard	

1. Place the Swiss cheese, Cheddar cheese, nutmeg, dry mustard, garlic, and flour in the pot. Stir to combine. Pour in the beer and stir well. 2. Cover with the lid and turn the dial to Slow Cook, cook on low for 2 hours, or until the cheese is melted. If you can, stir the mixture occasionally as the cheese melts. 3. Uncover and stir well. Serve the fondue right from the pot.

Per Serving: Calories 254; Fat 18. 99g; Sodium 211mg; Carbs 4. 72g; Fiber 0. 1g; Sugar 1. 27g; Protein 16. 06g

Sweet Carrots and Peppers

Prep time: 15 minutes | **Cook time:** 7-8 hours | **Serves:** 7

¼ cup low-sugar apricot preserves	1 red onion, sliced
2 tablespoons brown sugar	1 yellow bell pepper, seeded and sliced
1 tablespoon light whipped butter	1 green pepper, stem removed, seeded, and sliced
1 teaspoon cinnamon	1 tablespoon cornstarch
¼ teaspoon ground nutmeg	2 tablespoons cold water
2 pounds carrots, peeled and chopped	

1. Mix together the preserves, brown sugar, cinnamon, butter, and nutmeg in a small bowl. Then, add the carrots, onion, and bell peppers to the pot and pour in the glaze. Stir everything well to make sure the vegetables are coated with the glaze. 2. Cover with the lid and turn the dial to Slow Cook, cook on low for 7 to 8 hours, or on high for 3 to 4 hours. 3. After the vegetables are cooked, mix the cornstarch with water in a separate bowl and stir it until the cornstarch dissolves. Then add the mixture to the pot and mix it thoroughly. 4. Press START/STOP to stop cooking and leave uncovered until the sauce has thickened, about 15 minutes. Stir and enjoy.

Per Serving: Calories 107; Fat 2. 08g; Sodium 104mg; Carbs 22. 24g; Fiber 4. 4g; Sugar 12. 32g; Protein 1. 7g

Classic Caponata

Prep time: 10 minutes | Cook time: 8 hours | Serves: 8

1 large eggplant, peeled and cubed	½ cup golden raisins
2 (14-ounce) cans diced tomatoes, drained	¼ cup tomato paste
2 yellow onions, chopped	2 tablespoons freshly squeezed lemon juice
4 celery stalks, sliced	1 teaspoon dried Italian seasoning
2 red bell peppers, seeded and chopped	1 teaspoon sea salt
6 garlic cloves, sliced	⅛ teaspoon freshly ground black pepper

1. Place all of the ingredients in the pot. Stir well to combine. 2. Cover with the lid and turn the dial to Slow Cook, cook on low for 8 hours, or until the vegetables are tender and a sauce has formed. 3. Stir gently and serve.

Per Serving: Calories 112; Fat 2. 91g; Sodium 456mg; Carbs 21. 63g; Fiber 5. 6g; Sugar 14. 03g; Protein 2. 86g

Simple Candied Pecans

Prep time: 10 minutes | Cook time: 3 hours | Serves: 6

8 tablespoons (1 stick) butter, melted	1 teaspoon sea salt
¼ cup brown sugar	1 pound whole untoasted pecans
1 teaspoon hot sauce	

1. Combine the butter, brown sugar, hot sauce, and salt in a large bowl, mix well. Stir in the pecans and toss until well coated. 2. Transfer the pecan mixture to the pot. 3. Cover with the lid and turn the dial to Slow Cook, cook on low for 3 hours, stirring every 30 minutes to keep the pecans from burning. 4. Distribute the mixture evenly onto a spacious baking tray and allow it to reach room temperature. 5. Keep the pecans in an enclosed receptacle at room temperature for a maximum of 7 days.

Per Serving: Calories 693; Fat 69. 77g; Sodium 518mg; Carbs 19. 54g; Fiber 7. 3g; Sugar 11. 94g; Protein 7. 12g

Balsamic Brussels Sprouts and Cranberry

Prep time: 10 minutes | **Cook time:** 4½ hours | **Serves:** 4

1 tablespoon stone-ground mustard	⅓ cup dried cranberries, chopped
1 tablespoon extra-virgin olive oil	⅛ teaspoon freshly ground black pepper
¼ cup water	Pinch paprika
1 pound Brussels sprouts, trimmed and halved	½ cup balsamic vinegar
4 garlic cloves	

1. Whisk together mustard, olive oil, and water in a bowl until well combined. 2. Combine Brussels sprouts, garlic, and dried cranberries in the pot. Pour the mustard dressing over them and mix well to cover. Season with salt, black pepper, and paprika. 3. Cover with the lid, turn the dial to Slow Cook and cook on high for 2 hours and 15 minutes or on low for 4½ hours, or until the sprouts are tender and lightly browned. 4. Add the vinegar to a small pot, and bring to a boil. Reduce to a simmer and cook, stirring frequently, until it thickens to a syrup-like consistency, about 12 minutes. 5. Stir the sprouts and drizzle with the balsamic reduction. Serve immediately.

Per Serving: Calories 114; Fat 2. 46g; Sodium 67mg; Carbs 19. 92g; Fiber 4. 6g; Sugar 9. 88g; Protein 4. 62g

Spiced Mixed Nuts

Prep time: 10 minutes | **Cook time:** 1-2 hours | **Serves:** 8

4 cups raw, unsalted mixed nuts (almonds, cashews, pecans, etc.)	¼ teaspoon ground nutmeg
1 teaspoon ground cinnamon	⅓ cup pure maple syrup
¼ teaspoon ground ginger	1 teaspoon vanilla extract
	Zest of 1 orange

1. Mix together the nuts, ginger, cinnamon, and nutmeg in a medium bowl. 2. Add the maple syrup, orange zest, vanilla and toss thoroughly to coat. 3. Spray the pot with nonstick cooking spray. Add the spiced nut mixture. Cover with the lid and turn the dial to Slow Cook, cook on low for 1½ hours, stirring every 15 minutes. 4. Press START/STOP to stop cooking and spread the nuts onto waxed paper to cool completely.

Per Serving: Calories 444; Fat 36. 19g; Sodium 185mg; Carbs 23. 42g; Fiber 5g; Sugar 10. 72g; Protein 13. 47g

Juicy Honey–Soy Chicken Wings

Prep time: 10 minutes | **Cook time:** 8 hours | **Serves:** 6

¼ cup honey	1 teaspoon garlic powder
¼ cup low-sodium soy sauce	2 pounds chicken wings
Juice of 1 orange	1 teaspoon sesame seeds
1 tablespoon grated fresh ginger	3 scallions, thinly sliced

1. Mix together the honey, orange juice, soy sauce, ginger, and garlic powder in a small bowl. 2. Put the chicken wings in the pot. Pour the sauce over the wings and stir to coat. 3. Cover with the lid and turn the dial to Slow Cook, cook on low for 8 hours. 4. Serve garnished with the sesame seeds and scallions.

Per Serving: Calories 254; Fat 5. 71g; Sodium 508mg; Carbs 14. 89g; Fiber 0. 4g; Sugar 13. 07g; Protein 34. 66g

Spiced Nuts

Prep time: 10 minutes | **Cook time:** 4 hours | **Serves:** 6

Nonstick cooking spray	¼ teaspoon ground nutmeg
2 tablespoons honey	½ teaspoon sea salt
1 tablespoon olive oil	⅛ teaspoon cayenne pepper
Zest of 1 orange	1 cup unsalted raw pecans (or other raw nuts of your
1 teaspoon ground cinnamon	choice)
½ teaspoon ground ginger	

1. Spray the pot with nonstick cooking spray. 2. Mix together the honey, olive oil, ginger, nutmeg, orange zest, sea salt, cinnamon, and cayenne in a small bowl. 3. Add the nuts to the pot. Pour the spice mixture over the top. 4. Cover with the lid and turn the dial to Slow Cook, cook on low for 4 hours. 5. Turn off the pot. Remove the lid and allow the nuts to cool and harden for 2 hours, stirring occasionally to keep the nuts coated.

Per Serving: Calories 176; Fat 16. 14g; Sodium 194mg; Carbs 8. 99g; Fiber 2g; Sugar 6. 71g; Protein 1. 77g

Creamy French Onion Dip

Prep time: 10 minutes | **Cook time:** 9 hours | **Serves:** 8

3 onions, thinly sliced	⅛ teaspoon freshly ground black pepper
3 tablespoons olive oil	¾ cup fat-free sour cream
1 teaspoon dried thyme	¾ cup fat-free cream cheese, softened
½ teaspoon sea salt	Pinch cayenne pepper

1. Add the onions, olive oil, thyme, salt, and pepper to the pot and stir well to coat. 2. Cover with the lid and turn the dial to Slow Cook, cook on low for 8 hours. 3. First, take off the cover from the pot and increase the heat to the highest setting. Then, keep cooking while stirring every now and then until the liquid has almost disappeared, which should take 1 to 2 hours. 4. After that, leave the onions to cool for an hour. Lastly, mix the sour cream, cream cheese, and cayenne pepper together in a small bowl, and using a hand mixer is recommended for this step. 5. Stir in the onions and serve.

Per Serving: Calories 91; Fat 5. 34g; Sodium 366mg; Carbs 5. 81g; Fiber 0. 1g; Sugar 1. 71g; Protein 4. 95g

Lemony Spinach and Artichoke Dip

Prep time: 10 minutes | **Cook time:** 4 hours | **Serves:** 10

2 (14-ounce) cans artichoke hearts, drained and chopped	2 cups fat-free sour cream
2 cups baby spinach, stemmed	Zest of 1 lemon
½ red onion, minced	¼ teaspoon sea salt
3 garlic cloves, minced	¼ teaspoon freshly ground black pepper
8 ounces fat-free cream cheese	Pinch cayenne pepper

1. Combine all the ingredients in the pot. 2. Cover with the lid and turn the dial to Slow Cook, cook on low for 4 hours.

Per Serving: Calories 77; Fat 0. 36g; Sodium 302mg; Carbs 13. 19g; Fiber 2. 3g; Sugar 2. 05g; Protein 5. 99g

Spiced Cranberry–Apple Cider

Prep time: 10 minutes | **Cook time:** 1 hour | **Serves:** 8

4 cups apple cider

4 cups cranberry juice

4 cinnamon sticks

2 orange wedges

1 teaspoon whole cloves

1. Add the apple cider, cranberry juice, and cinnamon sticks to the pot. 2. Insert the cloves into the orange wedges and then include the pierced orange wedges in the pot. 3. Cover with the lid and turn the dial to Slow Cook, cook on high for 1 hour, or until the mixture is hot and steaming. 4. Remove the lid, reduce the heat to low, and ladle the warm cider into mugs. Discard the orange wedges before serving.

Per Serving: Calories 101; Fat 0. 26g; Sodium 3mg; Carbs 25. 86g; Fiber 1. 9g; Sugar 20. 73g; Protein 0. 24g

Chapter 4 Soup, Salad and Stew Recipes

Traditional Vegetable Broth

Prep time: 10 minutes | **Cook time:** 8-10 hours | **Serves:** 8 cups

2 tablespoons olive oil	4 cloves garlic
2 onions, chopped	1 teaspoon salt
3 carrots, chopped	¼ teaspoon white pepper
2 tomatoes, sliced	7 cups water
3 stalks celery, sliced	

1. Use the dial to select Sear/Sauté. Press the +/- TEMP buttons to choose LO temperature. press START/ STOP to begin cooking. 2. Heat the olive oil in the pot and add the onions and carrots; cook and stir until vegetables begin to brown. 3. Transfer to a bowl and set aside. Add 1 cup water to drippings remaining in the pot; bring to a boil; boil for 1 minute, stirring to loosen drippings in bottom of the pot. Press START/ STOP to turn off the Sear/Sauté function. 4. Add remaining ingredients to the pot. Cover with the lid and turn the dial to Slow Cook, cook on low for 8–10 hours. 5. Strain broth, discarding vegetables. Let the broth cool for 30 minutes, then strain into freezer containers and seal. Freeze up to 3 months. To thaw, let stand in refrigerator overnight.

Per Serving: Calories 54; Fat 3. 48g; Sodium 317mg; Carbs 5. 64g; Fiber 1. 3g; Sugar 2. 45g; Protein 0. 7g

Cheese Chicken and Pasta Stew

Prep time: 10 minutes | **Cook time:** 4-5 hours | **Serves:** 4

2 cups tomato juice	½ teaspoon hot sauce
3 cups water	3 tablespoons potato flakes
1 cup cooked ground chicken	1 cup small pasta
2 cups cooked vegetables	1 cup shredded Cheddar cheese

1. Mix together the tomato juice, water, and meat in the pot. Cover with the lid and turn the dial to Slow Cook, cook on low for 4–5 hours until hot. 2. Add remaining ingredients except cheese and turn pot to high. Cover and cook for 15–20 minutes or until stew is thickened and pasta is tender. Stir in cheese, and serve warm.

Per Serving: Calories 475; Fat 15. 12g; Sodium 385mg; Carbs 62. 67g; Fiber 10. 1g; Sugar 5. 31g; Protein 23. 81g

Cheese Bread Onion Soup

Prep time: 10 minutes | **Cook time:** 5 hours | **Serves:** 6

1 tablespoon vegetable oil	3 cups chicken stock
3 tablespoons butter, divided	2 cups beef stock
4 large onions, chopped	1 cup water
3 cloves garlic, minced	6 slices French bread, toasted
½ cup dry white wine	⅓ cup grated Parmesan cheese
1 tablespoon dried thyme leaves	1 cup grated Gruyere cheese
½ teaspoon pepper	

1. Use the dial to select Sear/Sauté. Press the +/- TEMP buttons to choose HI temperature. Press START/ STOP to begin cooking. Heat oil and 1 tablespoon butter in the pot. Add onions and garlic. Cook, stirring every hour, until onions begin to turn brown, about 4–5 minutes. 2. Add the wine, thyme, and pepper and stir well. Press START/STOP to turn off the Sear/Sauté function. 3. Then add both kinds of stock and water, cover, and turn the dial to Slow Cook, cook on high for 2–3 hours until soup is blended. 4. To prepare the dish, start by preheating the broiler. Then, take the French bread and spread 2 tablespoons of the remaining butter on it. Next, in a small bowl, mix together the cheeses and sprinkle the mixture over the bread. 5. Afterwards, pour the soup into bowls that are safe for the oven and put a slice of bread on top of each serving. 6. Place the bowls on a sturdy baking sheet and slide them under the broiler. Cook for 2 to 3 minutes or until the cheese starts to bubble and turn brown. Serve the dish immediately.

Per Serving: Calories 687; Fat 23. 64g; Sodium 1620mg; Carbs 88. 61g; Fiber 4. 9g; Sugar 13. 33g; Protein 31g

Split Pea and Potato Soup

Prep time: 10 minutes | **Cook time:** 8-9 hours | **Serves:** 6

2 tablespoons vegetable oil	1 teaspoon Worcestershire sauce
1 onion, chopped	½ teaspoon Tabasco sauce
3 carrots, sliced	1 bay leaf
3 celery stalks, sliced	2 cups dried green split peas, rinsed
2 cloves garlic, minced	8 cups water
½ teaspoon dried thyme leaves	1 pound potatoes, peeled and diced
¼ teaspoon pepper	1 teaspoon salt

1. Combine all ingredients in the pot. Cover with the lid and turn the dial to Slow Cook, cook on low for 8–9 hours or until peas and potatoes are tender. 2. Using a potato masher, partially mash some of the peas and potatoes. Re-cover the pot and cook on high for 10–15 minutes more or until soup is thickened and blended. Serve right away.

Per Serving: Calories 188; Fat 4. 92g; Sodium 571mg; Carbs 29. 84g; Fiber 7. 6g; Sugar 3. 64g; Protein 7. 34g

Creamy Mayo–Chicken and Celery Salad

Prep time: 10 minutes | **Cook time:** 6-7 hours | **Serves:** 4

5 boneless, skinless chicken breasts	2 cloves garlic, minced
½ teaspoon salt	½ cup mayonnaise
⅛ teaspoon pepper	⅓ cup sour cream
½ teaspoon dried thyme leaves	2 tablespoons milk
½ cup chicken stock	½ cup chopped celery
1 onion, chopped	2 tablespoons chopped parsley

1. Combine the chicken, salt, pepper, onion, thyme, chicken stock, and garlic in the pot. Cover with the lid and turn the dial to Slow Cook, cook on low for 6–7 hours or until chicken is thoroughly cooked. 2. Take a big bowl and mix all the ingredients that are left until they become smooth. Take the chicken out of the pot and cut it into 1-inch cubes. 3. Add the chicken to the bowl with the dressing as you work. Use a slotted spoon to remove the onions from the pot and add them to the chicken mixture. 4. Mix everything together gently, cover the bowl, and refrigerate it for 3-4 hours before serving.

Per Serving: Calories 509; Fat 19. 97g; Sodium 730mg; Carbs 7. 46g; Fiber 1. 2g; Sugar 2. 59g; Protein 70. 4g

Chicken, Veggie and Noodles Soup

Prep time: 10 minutes | **Cook time:** 8-9 hours | **Serves:** 8

2 tablespoons vegetable oil	3 stalks celery, chopped
8 bone-in chicken thighs	4 carrots, peeled and sliced
2 tablespoons flour	1 bay leaf
1 teaspoon salt, divided	1 teaspoon dried thyme leaves
¼ teaspoon pepper, divided	3 cups chicken stock
1 onion, chopped	5 cups water
4 cloves garlic, minced	2 cups egg noodles

1. Use the dial to select Sear/Sauté. Press the +/- TEMP buttons to choose LO temperature. Allow the unit to heat up for 5-minutes. 2. Heat the oil in the pot. Sprinkle chicken with flour, ½ teaspoon salt, and ⅛ teaspoon pepper, and place, skin side down, in the hot oil. Cook until browned, about 4–6 minutes, then remove from the pot and set aside. 3. To drippings remaining in the pot, add onion and garlic; cook and stir, scraping up the drippings, until crisp tender, about 4 minutes. Press START/STOP to turn off the Sear/Sauté function. 4. Add chicken and all remaining ingredients except egg noodles to the pot. Cover with the lid and turn the dial to Slow Cook, cook on low for 8–9 hours or until chicken and vegetables are tender. 5. Take out the chicken from the pot, remove the skin and bones, and tear the meat into small pieces. Put the chicken pieces back into the soup. 6. Increase the heat and add egg noodles to the soup. Cover and let the noodles cook for 10-15 minutes or the dumplings cook for 20-25 minutes until they are fully cooked. 7. Finally, remove the bay leaf and serve the soup immediately.

Per Serving: Calories 562; Fat 37. 43g; Sodium 588mg; Carbs 17. 54g; Fiber 1g; Sugar 2. 41g; Protein 36. 51g

Spinach and Beets Borscht

Prep time: 10 minutes | Cook time: 6-7 hours | Serves: 5

4 slices bacon	½ teaspoon salt
1 onion, chopped	⅛ teaspoon pepper
3 cloves garlic, minced	1 tablespoon apple cider vinegar
2 (15-ounce) cans sliced beets	2 cups spinach leaves, chopped
1 (6-ounce) can tomato paste	½ cup sour cream
3 cups chicken stock	¼ cup chopped parsley
½ teaspoon dill seed	

1. Turn dial to Sear/Sauté, set temperature to /LO, and press START/STOP to begin cooking. Add the bacon to the pot and cook bacon until crisp; remove bacon to paper towel to drain; crumble and refrigerate. In drippings remaining in the pot, cook onion and garlic until tender, about 5 minutes. Press START/STOP to turn off the Sear/Sauté function. 2. Then, add beets, chicken stock, dill seed, tomato paste, salt, and pepper to the pot. Cover with the lid and turn the dial to Slow Cook, cook on low for 6-7 hours until vegetables are soft. 3. Using an immersion blender or potato masher, mash some of the beets, leaving some whole. Stir in apple cider vinegar. 4. Separate the spinach leaves into six soup bowls and then pour hot soup over the spinach. Finally, add some sour cream, reserved bacon, and parsley as garnish.
Per Serving: Calories 261; Fat 12. 83g; Sodium 671mg; Carbs 27. 66g; Fiber 5. 3g; Sugar 15. 32g; Protein 11. 24g

Yogurt Beef and Potato Salad

Prep time: 10 minutes | Cook time: 8-9 hours | Serves: 4

¾ pound sirloin tip	1 jalapeño pepper, minced
2 teaspoons chili powder	1 (16-ounce) jar mild salsa
½ teaspoon salt	½ cup mayonnaise
⅛ teaspoon pepper	⅓ cup plain yogurt
3 potatoes, peeled and cubed	1 green bell pepper, chopped
1 onion, chopped	½ cup cubed pepper jack cheese
2 cloves garlic, minced	¼ cup chopped fresh cilantro

1. Cut sirloin into 1-inch pieces. Sprinkle with chili powder, salt, and pepper. Place potatoes, onions, garlic, and jalapeño in the bottom of the pot. Add the beef on top. 2. Pour half of the salsa over all. Cover and turn the dial to Slow Cook, cook on low for 8–9 hours or until beef and potatoes are tender. 3. Combine the leftover salsa, mayonnaise, bell pepper, yogurt, and cheese in a large bowl and mix well. Use a large slotted spoon or sieve to remove the hot beef mixture from the pot and add it to the bowl. Stir gently to coat and discard the liquid left in the pot. 4. Refrigerate the mixture for 4-5 hours until it is cold. Before serving, stir it gently and top it with cilantro.
Per Serving: Calories 544; Fat 20. 77g; Sodium 1828mg; Carbs 71. 07g; Fiber 11g; Sugar 12. 24g; Protein 22. 21g

Chicken, Wild Rice and Red Grape Salad

Prep time: 10 minutes | **Cook time:** 6-7 hours | **Serves:** 5

1 cup wild rice	½ cup apple juice
1 onion, chopped	¾ cup mayonnaise
3 boneless, skinless chicken breasts, cubed	½ cup yogurt
2 cups chicken stock	¼ cup apple juice
½ teaspoon salt	1 cup seedless red grapes
¼ teaspoon pepper	2 stalks celery, chopped
1 teaspoon dried thyme leaves	

1. Combine the wild rice and onion in the pot. Spread the chicken on top. Sprinkle with salt, pepper, and thyme, then pour the stock and ¼ apple juice over all. 2. Cover with the lid and turn the dial to Slow Cook, cook on low for 6–7 hours or until wild rice is tender and chicken is cooked. 3. Get a big bowl and mix together mayonnaise, yogurt, and apple juice. 4. Take the chicken mixture out of the pot using a large spoon with holes or a strainer, and add it to the mayonnaise mixture along with the other ingredients. 5. Cover the bowl and put it in the fridge for 3 to 4 hours, until it's cold. Before you serve it, give it a light stir.
Per Serving: Calories 913; Fat 27. 3g; Sodium 893mg; Carbs 38. 39g; Fiber 3. 3g; Sugar 11. 64g; Protein 122. 6g

Red Snapper and Potato Salad

Prep time: 10 minutes | **Cook time:** 8½-9½ hours | **Serves:** 5

4 russet potatoes	¼ pound frozen small cooked shrimp, thawed
1 onion, chopped	1½ cups frozen peas
2 cloves garlic, minced	½ cup mayonnaise
½ teaspoon salt	½ cup plain yogurt
⅛ teaspoon white pepper	¼ cup seafood cocktail sauce
2 cups water	¼ cup whole milk
¼ pound red snapper fish fillets	

1. Peel the potatoes and cut into cubes, place in the pot and stir in the onions and garlic. Sprinkle with salt and pepper, then pour water over all. 2. Cover with the lid and turn the dial to Slow Cook, cook on low for 8–9 hours or until potatoes are tender. 3. Increase the heat to the HIGH setting. Put the red snapper fillets on top of the potato mixture. Cover the pot and cook for around 30 minutes or until the fish can be easily flaked with a fork. 4. Take a big bowl and mix the rest of the ingredients thoroughly. Using a large slotted spoon or a sieve, take out the fish and potato mixture from the pot and add it to the mixture in the bowl. 5. Gently stir the mixture to coat everything well. Cover the bowl and keep it in the refrigerator for about 4 to 5 hours until it's cold. 6. Before serving, gently stir the mixture once again.
Per Serving: Calories 416; Fat 10. 4g; Sodium 618mg; Carbs 66. 04g; Fiber 6. 4g; Sugar 6. 59g; Protein 16. 73g

Creamy Wild Rice and Cauliflower Chowder

Prep time: 10 minutes | Cook time: 10-11 hours | Serves: 6

1 tablespoon olive oil	3 carrots, sliced
1 tablespoon butter	2 cups chicken stock
1 onion, chopped	3 cups water
4 cloves garlic, minced	1½ cups frozen corn
½ teaspoon salt	2 cups frozen cauliflower florets
⅛ teaspoon white pepper	½ cup light cream
½ teaspoon dried tarragon leaves	3 tablespoons cornstarch
½ cup wild rice, rinsed	1 cup shredded Swiss cheese

1. Heat olive oil and butter in a big saucepan on medium heat. Add onion and garlic, and stir and cook until they become crisp and tender, which should take approximately 4 minutes. 2. Place wild rice in the pot and sprinkle with salt, pepper, and tarragon. Add the onion mixture, carrots, stock, and water. Cover with the lid and turn the dial to Slow Cook, cook on low for 8–9 hours or until wild rice is tender. 3. Add corn and cauliflower to pot and cook on low for 2 hours longer. in a small bowl, mix cream and cornstarch thoroughly. 4. Add this mixture to the pot and cook on high heat for 5-10 minutes until the soup thickens. Finally, add cheese and stir well before serving.

Per Serving: Calories 643; Fat 23. 54g; Sodium 489mg; Carbs 29. 31g; Fiber 3. 2g; Sugar 4. 39g; Protein 75. 63g

Vegetable, Beef and Barley Stew

Prep time: 10 minutes | Cook time: 8-9 hours | Serves: 8

¾ pound beef round steak	3 potatoes, cubed
2 tablespoons flour	1 (8-ounce) package sliced mushrooms
1 teaspoon salt	4 cups water
1 teaspoon paprika	1 teaspoon dried marjoram leaves
2 tablespoons olive oil	1 bay leaf
2 onions, chopped	¼ teaspoon pepper
3 cups beef stock, divided	¾ cup hulled barley
4 carrots, thickly sliced	

1. Trim beef and cut into 1-inch pieces. Sprinkle with flour, salt, and paprika and toss to coat. Turn dial to Sear/Sauté, set temperature to LO, and press START/STOP to begin cooking. Heat the olive oil in the pot. Add the beef, stirring occasionally, cook for about 5–6 minutes. 2. Add onions and ½ cup beef stock. Bring to a boil, then simmer, scraping the bottom of the skillet, for 3–4 minutes. Add all remaining ingredients to the pot. Press START/STOP to turn off the Sear/Sauté function. 3. Cover with the lid and turn the dial to Slow Cook, cook on low for 8–9 hours, or until barley and vegetables are tender. Stir, remove bay leaf, and serve right away.

Per Serving: Calories 290; Fat 5. 53g; Sodium 510mg; Carbs 44. 44g; Fiber 6. 7g; Sugar 3. 08g; Protein 16. 47g

Lentil and Carrot Stew

Prep time: 10 minutes | **Cook time:** 7-8 hours | **Serves:** 6

1 onion, chopped	1½ cups brown lentils
3 cloves garlic, minced	½ teaspoon salt
3 carrots, sliced	¼ teaspoon pepper
½ teaspoon dried thyme leaves	1 (14-ounce) can diced tomatoes, undrained
4 cups vegetable broth	¼ cup chopped flat-leaf parsley
2 cups water	¼ cup grated Parmesan cheese

1. Mix together the onion, garlic, carrots, thyme, Broth, water, lentils, salt, and pepper in the pot. Cover with the lid and turn the dial to Slow Cook. Cook on low for 7–8 hours or until lentils are tender. 2. Add tomatoes and stir. Cover and cook on high heat for 20–30 minutes more or until stew is hot and blended. Spread parsley and cheese on top and serve.

Per Serving: Calories 62; Fat 1. 52g; Sodium 360mg; Carbs 10. 13g; Fiber 2. 2g; Sugar 2. 79g; Protein 4. 05g

Sausage, Corn and Potato Stew

Prep time: 10 minutes | **Cook time:** 8-9 hours | **Serves:** 8

2 slices bacon	2 cups water
½ pound Polish sausage	2 cups frozen corn
1 onion, chopped	1 (13-ounce) can evaporated milk
3 cloves garlic, minced	2 tablespoons cornstarch
3 potatoes, peeled and cubed	¼ cup chopped chives
4 cups chicken stock	

1. Turn dial to Sear/Sauté, set temperature to LO, and press START/STOP to begin cooking. Add the bacon and cook until crisp. Drain on paper towels, crumble, and refrigerate. Cut sausage into 1-inch slices and cook for 2–3 minutes in bacon drippings. 2. Add onion and garlic, cook and stir for 4 minutes. Press START/STOP to turn off the Sear/Sauté function. Add potatoes, stock, frozen corn and water. 3. Cover with the lid and turn the dial to Slow Cook, cook on low for 8 hours. In small bowl, combine cornstarch and evaporated milk; mix well. Add to pot along with reserved bacon. 4. Cover and cook on high for 30–40 minutes more, or until stew is thickened. Sprinkle with chives and serve.

Per Serving: Calories 360; Fat 14. 4g; Sodium 484mg; Carbs 43. 96g; Fiber 4. 3g; Sugar 7. 31g; Protein 13. 72g

Thyme Corn & Potato Chowder

Prep time: 10 minutes | Cook time: 6 hours | Serves: 2

2 cups frozen corn kernels, thawed, divided	1 thyme sprig
½ cup diced onion	⅛ teaspoon sea salt
1 garlic clove, minced	2 tablespoons heavy cream (optional)
3 Yukon Gold potatoes, peeled and diced	1 scallion, white and green parts, sliced thin, for garnish
2 cups low-sodium chicken broth	

1. Add 1½ cups of corn kernels, potatoes, the onion, garlic, thyme, broth, and salt to the pot, stir well. Cover with the lid and turn the dial to Slow Cook, cook on low for 6 hours. 2. Remove the thyme sprig and add the heavy cream (if using) to the pot. Purée the soup with an immersion blender until it is smooth. 3. Add the remaining ½ cup of corn kernels and scallions to each serving as a garnish.

Per Serving: Calories 716; Fat 9. 54g; Sodium 273mg; Carbs 139. 93g; Fiber 16. 5g; Sugar 11. 08g; Protein 21. 87g

Thai–Style Eggplant & Mushroom Curry Soup

Prep time: 10 minutes | Cook time: 6-8 hours | Serves: 2

1 small eggplant, cut into 1-inch cubes, about 2 cups	1 cup coconut milk
1 teaspoon sea salt	2 cups low-sodium chicken broth
1 cup quartered button mushrooms	1 tablespoon Thai red curry paste
1 onion, halved and sliced in thick half-circles	1 tablespoon freshly squeezed lime juice
1 red bell pepper, cut into long strips	¼ cup fresh cilantro, for garnish

1. Place the eggplant in a colander over the sink and sprinkle it with salt. Let it sit for 10 minutes or up to 30 minutes if you have more time. 2. Combine mushrooms, red bell pepper, onion, broth, coconut milk, and red curry paste in the pot. 3. Rinse the eggplant in the colander and gently squeeze out any extra moisture from each cube. Then, add the eggplant to the pot and mix all ingredients together. 4. Cover with the lid and turn the dial to Slow Cook, cook on low for 6 to 8 hours. 5. Stir in the lime juice and garnish each serving with the cilantro, serve.

Per Serving: Calories 157; Fat 6. 23g; Sodium 1295mg; Carbs 17. 56g; Fiber 3. 9g; Sugar 10. 49g; Protein 11. 52g

Healthy Chicken and White Bean Soup

Prep time: 10 minutes | **Cook time:** 5-7 hours | **Serves:** 4

1½ pounds chicken breasts, boneless and skinless, cut into 1-inch chunks	3 garlic cloves, minced
	2 dried bay leaves
1 pound white beans, soaked overnight	1 teaspoon dried basil
1 (15-ounce) can no-salt-added diced tomatoes	1 teaspoon dried oregano
4 cups low-sodium chicken	1 teaspoon dried thyme
3 carrots, diced	Salt
2 celery stalks, diced	Freshly ground black pepper
1 large onion, diced	

1. Add the chicken, carrots, beans, tomatoes and their juices, broth, garlic, bay leaves, celery, onion, oregano, basil, and thyme, and a small amount of salt and pepper to the pot. Stir to mix well. 2. Cover with the lid and turn the dial to Slow Cook, cook on low for 5 to 7 hours. 3. Remove the bay leaves and serve warm.

Per Serving: Calories 415; Fat 18. 2g; Sodium 379mg; Carbs 21. 19g; Fiber 6. 7g; Sugar 7. 97g; Protein 43. 58g

Chicken and Black Bean Soup

Prep time: 10 minutes | **Cook time:** 5-7 hours | **Serves:** 4

5 cups low-sodium chicken broth	2 teaspoons ground cumin
1 pound boneless, skinless chicken breasts	1 teaspoon paprika
1 pound dry black beans, soaked overnight	½ teaspoon ground coriander
1-pound corn kernels, fresh or frozen	Juice of 1 lime
1 (15-ounce) can no-salt-added diced tomatoes	Salt
1 onion, diced	Freshly ground black pepper
3 garlic cloves, minced	¼ cup chopped fresh cilantro
1 tablespoon chili powder	

1. Add the broth, chicken breasts, corn, beans, onion, garlic, tomatoes and their juices, paprika, chili powder, coriander, cumin, lime juice, salt and pepper to the pot, stir well. 2. Cover with the lid and turn the dial to Slow Cook, cook on low for 5 to 7 hours. 3. Put the chicken onto a plate, use two forks to break it into small pieces, and then put it back into the pot. 4. Add some cilantro on top before serving.

Per Serving: Calories 759; Fat 12. 35g; Sodium 856mg; Carbs 125. 13g; Fiber 25. 7g; Sugar 16. 1g; Protein 45. 59g

Barley and Chickpea Stew

Prep time: 10 minutes | Cook time: 4-6 hours | Serves: 4

Nonstick cooking spray
1½ cups uncooked barley, rinsed
1 (15-ounce) can chickpeas, drained and rinsed
3 cups water
2 garlic cloves, minced
1 onion, minced

1 teaspoon salt
½ teaspoon dried rosemary
½ teaspoon freshly ground black pepper
¼ cup grated Parmesan cheese
¼ cup chopped fresh parsley

1. Spray the pot with nonstick cooking spray. 2. Add the barley, chickpeas, garlic, onion, water, salt, pepper, rosemary, and cheese to the pot. Stir to mix well. 3. Cover with the lid and turn the dial to Slow Cook, cook on low for 4 to 6 hours. 4. Top with fresh parsley before serving.

Per Serving: Calories 393; Fat 4. 26g; Sodium 843mg; Carbs 77. 2g; Fiber 16. 4g; Sugar 4. 36g; Protein 14. 22g

Turkey, Wild Rice and Veggie Soup

Prep time: 10 minutes | Cook time: 6-8 hours | Serves: 6

6 cups low-sodium chicken broth or water
¾ pound boneless, skinless turkey, chopped
1 cup uncooked wild rice
1 small onion, chopped
3 celery stalks, diced
2 carrots, sliced

4 ounces mushrooms, sliced
¾ teaspoon salt
½ teaspoon freshly ground black pepper
1 dried bay leaf
1 teaspoon extra-virgin olive oil
Fresh rosemary, for garnish (optional)

1. Add the broth, turkey, rice, carrots, mushrooms, onion, celery, bay leaf, salt, pepper, and olive oil to the pot. Stir to mix well. 2. Cover with the lid and turn the dial to Slow Cook, cook on low for 6 to 8 hours. 3. Remove the bay leaf before serving, and add the rosemary as a garnish (if using).

Per Serving: Calories 247; Fat 5. 38g; Sodium 531mg; Carbs 36. 95g; Fiber 3. 1g; Sugar 5. 05g; Protein 14. 8g

Chapter 5 Poultry mains Recipes

Spicy Cheese Chicken & Tortilla Chips Casserole

Prep time: 10 minutes | **Cook time:** 8-9 hours | **Serves:** 6

2 cups tortilla chips
1 tablespoon vegetable oil
1 onion, chopped
2 cloves garlic, minced
2 slow-cooker simmered chicken breasts, chopped
1 (10-ounce) can condensed nacho cheese soup

1 (14-ounce) can diced tomatoes, undrained
1 (4-ounce) can chopped green chiles
1 tablespoon chili powder
⅛ teaspoon cayenne pepper
¾ cup shredded Cheddar cheese

1. Turn dial to Sear/Sauté, set temperature to LO, and press START/STOP to begin cooking. Heat the vegetable oil and cook onion and garlic until crisp-tender. Stir in chicken and cook for about 3 minutes. Press START/STOP to turn off the Sear/Sauté function. Transfer half of chicken mixture to a bowl. 2. Mix together the soup, green chiles, diced tomatoes, chili powder, and cayenne pepper in a large bowl and mix well. 3. Add tortilla chips, and soup mixture to the pot, then layer the other half chicken mixture. Cover with the lid and turn the dial to Slow Cook, cook on low for 8–9 hours or until casserole is bubbling around edges. 4. Sprinkle with cheese, cover, and let stand for 10 minutes before serving.
Per Serving: Calories 195; Fat 11. 25g; Sodium 598mg; Carbs 16. 9g; Fiber 3. 1g; Sugar 3. 23g; Protein 7. 85g

Cheesy Bacon–Wrapped Chicken Stew

Prep time: 10 minutes | **Cook time:** 6-8 hours | **Serves:** 4

4 boneless, skinless chicken breasts
½ teaspoon salt
⅛ teaspoon white pepper
½ teaspoon dried thyme leaves
4 thin slices boiled ham

1 onion, chopped
2 cloves garlic, minced
3 carrots, sliced
1 (10-ounce) can condensed chicken soup
1 cup shredded Swiss cheese

1. Add salt, pepper, and thyme to chicken breasts and then wrap a slice of ham around each breast, securing it with toothpicks. 2. Put onion, garlic, and carrots in a pot and place the wrapped chicken breasts on top. 3. Combine remaining ingredients in a bowl and pour into the pot. Cover with the lid and turn the dial to Slow Cook, cook on low for 6–8 hours or until chicken is thoroughly cooked. 4. Serve chicken and carrots with sauce.
Per Serving: Calories 590; Fat 22. 8g; Sodium 755mg; Carbs 5. 44g; Fiber 0. 6g; Sugar 1. 73g; Protein 86. 62g

Chicken and Pineapple Curry

Prep time: 10 minutes | **Cook time:** 6-8 hours | **Serves:** 4

3 boneless, skinless chicken breasts
1 onion, chopped
3 carrots, sliced
1 (8-ounce) can crushed pineapple, undrained
3 cloves garlic, minced
1 cup chicken stock
1 tablespoon curry powder

1 tablespoon grated gingerroot
½ teaspoon salt
⅛ teaspoon pepper
½ cup apple chutney
1 tablespoon cornstarch
¼ cup apple juice

1. Cut chicken into 1-inch pieces. Place onions, carrots, pineapple, and garlic in the pot. Top with chicken pieces. 2. Mix together the stock, gingerroot, curry powder, salt, and pepper. Pour into pot. 3. Cover with the lid and turn the dial to Slow Cook, cook on low for 6–8 hours or until vegetables are tender and chicken is thoroughly cooked. 4. Mix chutney, cornstarch, and apple juice in a small bowl, and then stir this mixture into the pot. 5. Cover and cook on high heat for 20-30 minutes. After that, stir everything well and serve it over hot cooked rice.

Per Serving: Calories 581; Fat 6. 42g; Sodium 489mg; Carbs 90. 48g; Fiber 5. 8g; Sugar 77. 23g; Protein 44. 56g

Apple–Bread Stuffed Chicken Rolls

Prep time: 10 minutes | **Cook time:** 5-7 hours | **Serves:** 4

2 slices oatmeal bread
⅓ cup finely chopped apple
¼ cup raisins
1 tablespoon lemon juice
2 tablespoons butter, melted
1 tablespoon sugar

½ teaspoon salt
4 boneless, skinless chicken breasts
1 onion, chopped
⅓ cup apple juice
½ teaspoon cinnamon

1. Toast the bread until it turns golden brown, then cut it into small cubes. Mix together some diced apples, raisins, lemon juice, melted butter, sugar, and salt in a medium-sized bowl. Add the bread cubes to the mixture and stir everything together. 2. Place the chicken breasts on a flat surface and gently pound them with a meat mallet or rolling pin until they are approximately ⅓ inch thick. Take the bread mixture and divide it equally among the chicken breasts. Roll up the chicken and use a toothpick to secure it. 3. Put the onions in a cooking pot, and place the filled chicken rolls on top. In a small bowl, combine apple juice and cinnamon, then spoon this mixture over the chicken. 4. Cover with the lid and turn the dial to Slow Cook, cook on low for 5 to 7 hours, or until chicken registers 165°F on food thermometer. 5. Remove toothpicks and serve chicken with the cooked onions.

Per Serving: Calories 405; Fat 12. 62g; Sodium 505mg; Carbs 15. 22g; Fiber 1. 4g; Sugar 7. 25g; Protein 54. 67g

Spicy Chicken Tacos

Prep time: 10 minutes | Cook time: 6-7 hours | Serves: 4

1 onion, chopped	½ cup chunky medium or hot salsa
4 cloves garlic, minced	1 (8-ounce) can tomato sauce
1 jalapeño pepper, minced	4 taco shells
2 boneless, skinless chicken breasts	1 cup grated Cheddar cheese
1 tablespoon chili powder	2 cups shredded lettuce
½ teaspoon salt	½ cup sour cream
⅛ teaspoon cayenne pepper	

1. Add onions, garlic, and jalapeño pepper to the pot, stir to mix well. Sprinkle chicken with chili powder, salt, and cayenne pepper; place on top of onions. 2. Pour salsa and tomato sauce over all. Cover with the lid and turn the dial to Slow Cook, cook on low for 6–7 hours or until chicken is thoroughly cooked. 3. Using two forks, shred chicken. Stir mixture in pot. 4. Heat the taco shells according to the instructions on the package and then offer the chicken filling, along with the taco shells and other ingredients, so that everyone can assemble their own tacos.

Per Serving: Calories 404; Fat 19. 09g; Sodium 950mg; Carbs 21. 01g; Fiber 4. 3g; Sugar 5. 32g; Protein 37. 5g

Lime Chicken and Brown Rice Casserole

Prep time: 10 minutes | Cook time: 5-7 hours | Serves: 6

Nonstick cooking spray	2 garlic cloves, minced
1 pound boneless, skinless chicken thighs	Juice of 2 limes
2 cups uncooked brown rice	1 teaspoon ground cumin
4 cups water	1 teaspoon salt
1 (15-ounce) can no-salt-added diced tomatoes	½ teaspoon freshly ground black pepper
1 (15-ounce) can black beans, drained and rinsed	½ teaspoon dried oregano
1 (15-ounce) can corn, drained and rinsed	½ cup chopped fresh cilantro

1. Spray the pot with nonstick cooking spray. 2. Add the chicken, rice, corn, tomatoes and their juices, water, beans, garlic, cumin, lime juice, salt, pepper, and oregano to the pot. Stir to mix well. 3. Cover and turn the dial to Slow Cook, cook on low for 5 to 7 hours, or until the rice is tender. 4. Sprinkle with fresh cilantro before serving.

Per Serving: Calories 449; Fat 6. 89g; Sodium 814mg; Carbs 85. 17g; Fiber 6. 8g; Sugar 9. 74g; Protein 14. 52g

Turkey and Beans Chili

Prep time: 10 minutes | Cook time: 4-6 hours | Serves: 4

2 pounds ground turkey
1 (28-ounce) can no-salt-added crushed tomatoes
1 (10-ounce) can no-salt-added diced tomatoes with green chiles
1 cup marinara sauce
1 (15-ounce) can red kidney beans, drained and rinsed
1 onion, chopped

3 garlic cloves, minced
2 tablespoons chili powder
2 teaspoons ground cumin
1½ teaspoons paprika
¼ teaspoon salt
1 teaspoon dried oregano

1. Turn dial to Sear/Sauté, set temperature to LO, and press START/STOP to begin cooking. Add the turkey and cook until browned, about 12 minutes, drain the fat. Press START/STOP to turn off the Sear/Sauté function. 2. Put the crushed tomatoes, diced tomatoes with chiles and their juices, beans, marinara sauce, chili powder, cumin, paprika, salt, onion, garlic, and oregano into the pot, and mix everything thoroughly by stirring. 3. Cover and turn the dial to Slow Cook, cook on low for 4 to 6 hours and serve.
Per Serving: Calories 485; Fat 22. 75g; Sodium 958mg; Carbs 23. 67g; Fiber 9g; Sugar 11. 32g; Protein 51. 15g

Chipotle–Peanut Butter Chicken and Potatoes

Prep time: 10 minutes | Cook time: 7-8 hours | Serves: 8

½ cup chicken stock or store-bought chicken stock
⅔ cup peanut butter
1 cup yellow onion, chopped
1 tablespoon jarred minced garlic
3 tablespoons lime juice
1 teaspoon ground ginger
1 teaspoon salt

2 chipotle chiles in adobo sauce, minced
2 tablespoons adobo sauce
2 pounds baby red potatoes
1-pound cauliflower florets
3 pounds boneless, skinless chicken thighs, cut into strips

1. Add the stock, peanut butter, lime juice, ginger, salt, onion, garlic, chipotle chiles, and adobo sauce to the pot and mix well. 2. Stir in the potatoes and cauliflower. Top with the chicken strips. 3. Cover with the lid and turn the dial to Slow Cook, cook on Low for 7 to 8 hours, or until the vegetables are tender and the chicken registers 165°F on a food thermometer. 4. You should keep any remaining food in the fridge with a cover on it, and it should not be frozen. This should be done for a maximum of 4 days.
Per Serving: Calories 614; Fat 22. 62g; Sodium 1294mg; Carbs 66. 09g; Fiber 6. 8g; Sugar 17. 3g; Protein 36. 78g

Turkey and Squash Stew

Prep time: 10 minutes | **Cook time:** 5-7 hours | **Serves:** 4

2 pounds spaghetti squash, cooked
1 pound cooked turkey, diced
1 small onion, diced
½ cup sliced mushrooms
3 garlic cloves, minced
1 teaspoon garlic powder
¼ teaspoon salt
½ teaspoon ground cumin
¾ teaspoon freshly ground black pepper, divided

½ teaspoon dried sage
½ teaspoon dried parsley
¼ teaspoon celery salt
1 tablespoon unsalted butter
1 tablespoon almond flour
¾ cup low-fat milk
1 cup low-fat mozzarella cheese, divided
2 tablespoons grated Parmesan cheese

1. Turn dial to Bake, set the temperature to 400°F. Set the time to 5 minutes and press START/STOP to begin preheating. 2. Halve the squash, and scrape out the seeds. Lay the squash halves cut-side down in the pot and cook for 30 to 45 minutes, until tender when pierced with a fork. Cool slightly. 3. Use a fork to break apart the spaghetti squash. Then, mix together turkey, mushrooms, onion, garlic, cumin, ½ teaspoon of pepper, garlic powder, salt, sage, parsley, and celery salt in the pot. Stir well. 4. In a medium-sized saucepan, melt the butter over medium heat. Add almond flour and stir until it starts to bubble. 5. Gradually pour in the milk while whisking continuously until it's completely combined. 6. Add ¼ teaspoon of pepper and stir. Slowly add ½ cup of mozzarella cheese while stirring constantly. 7. Keep whisking until the cheese is fully melted, which should take a few minutes. 8. Pour the sauce mixture into the pot, and stir again to mix well. Top with the Parmesan cheese. 9. Cover and turn the dial to Slow Cook, cook on low for 4 to 6 hours. 10. Sprinkle the remaining ½ cup of mozzarella cheese over the top, and cook for an additional 15 minutes on low, until the cheese melts, and serve.

Per Serving: Calories 512; Fat 22. 09g; Sodium 872mg; Carbs 27. 88g; Fiber 4g; Sugar 1. 15g; Protein 51. 63g

Maple–Balsamic Chicken and Potato

Prep time: 10 minutes | **Cook time:** 7-8 hours | **Serves:** 6

4 pounds boneless, skinless chicken thighs
1 teaspoon salt
1 teaspoon paprika
1 cup yellow onion, chopped
3 russet potatoes, cut into 1-inch-thick rounds

1 pound cubed sweet potatoes
¼ cup maple syrup
2 tablespoons balsamic vinegar
½ cup chicken stock or store-bought chicken stock

1. Sprinkle the chicken with the salt and paprika. 2. Add the onion, russet potatoes, and sweet potatoes to the pot. Spread chicken on top of the vegetables. 3. Drizzle everything, including the chicken, with the maple syrup, vinegar, and stock. 4. Cover with the lid and turn the dial to Slow Cook, cook on Low for 7 to 8 hours, or until the chicken registers 165°F on a food thermometer.

Per Serving: Calories 717; Fat 16. 44g; Sodium 753mg; Carbs 57. 61g; Fiber 4. 4g; Sugar 11. 15g; Protein 81. 31g

Chicken Caesar Pasta

Prep time: 10 minutes | **Cook time:** 7-8 hours | **Serves:** 8

1 tablespoon jarred minced garlic	1 (8-ounce) package sliced button mushrooms
2 teaspoons anchovy paste	1 cup prechopped yellow onion
2 tablespoons lemon juice	2 cups chicken stock or store-bought chicken stock
2 tablespoons Dijon mustard	1 cup water
1 cup buttermilk	1 (16-ounce) package uncooked ziti or mostaccioli
1 tablespoon cornstarch	pasta
3 pounds boneless, skinless chicken thighs, cut into strips	1 cup grated Parmesan cheese

1. Add the garlic, lemon juice, anchovy paste, and mustard to the pot and mix well. Stir in the buttermilk and cornstarch until combined. 2. Add the chicken, mushrooms, onion, stock, and water and stir. 3. Cover and turn the dial to Slow Cook, cook on Low for 7 to 8 hours, or until the chicken registers 165°F on a food thermometer. Turn the pot to High. 4. Stir in the pasta. Cover and cook for 20 to 25 minutes, or until the pasta is al dente. Stir in the cheese and serve. 5. Store leftovers covered in the refrigerator for up to 4 days or freeze for up to 2 months.

Per Serving: Calories 452; Fat 15. 82g; Sodium 905mg; Carbs 53. 26g; Fiber 4. 6g; Sugar 12. 18g; Protein 23. 41g

Simple Salsa Chicken

Prep time: 10 minutes | **Cook time:** 8 hours | **Serves:** 6

2 pounds boneless, skinless chicken thighs	2 cups red salsa (or store-bought)

1. Place the chicken in the pot and pour the salsa over it. 2. Cover with the lid and turn the dial to Slow Cook, cook on low for 8 hours or on high for 4 hours, until the chicken reads 165°F on a food thermometer.

Per Serving: Calories 288; Fat 8. 75g; Sodium 1015mg; Carbs 37. 41g; Fiber 3. 8g; Sugar 11. 52g; Protein 15. 35g

Lemony Chicken Stew

Prep time: 10 minutes | **Cook time:** 6-8 hours | **Serves:** 4

2 pounds boneless, skinless chicken thighs
½ teaspoon sea salt
⅛ teaspoon freshly ground black pepper
¼ cup freshly squeezed lemon juice

3 tablespoons capers, undrained
1 bay leaf
¾ cup chicken stock (or store-bought)

1. Season the chicken with the salt and pepper. Place the chicken, capers, lemon juice, bay leaf, and stock in the pot. Stir to mix well. 2. Cover with the lid and turn the dial to Slow Cook, cook on low for 6 to 8 hours or on high for 3 to 4 hours, until the chicken reads 165°F on a food thermometer. 3. Remove and discard the bay leaf before serving.

Per Serving: Calories 416; Fat 13. 55g; Sodium 1112mg; Carbs 50. 5g; Fiber 3. 7g; Sugar 13. 28g; Protein 22. 38g

Herbed Chicken Thighs with Grape Tomatoes

Prep time: 10 minutes | **Cook time:** 8 hours | **Serves:** 4

2 pints grape tomatoes
6 garlic cloves, minced
Grated zest of 1 lemon
1 tablespoon extra-virgin olive oil
4 (6-ounce) bone-in, skinless chicken thighs

2 teaspoons fresh thyme leaves
1 teaspoon fresh rosemary, chopped
¼ teaspoon sea salt
Freshly ground black pepper

1. Add the tomatoes, lemon zest, garlic, and olive oil to the pot. Gently stir to mix. 2. Place the chicken thighs on top of the tomato mixture and sprinkle them with thyme, rosemary, salt, and a small amount of ground black pepper. 3. Cover with the lid and turn the dial to Slow Cook, cook on low for 8 hours, or until the chicken is tender and reads at least 165°F on a food thermometer. Serve the chicken with the tomatoes and garlic.

Per Serving: Calories 470; Fat 31. 43g; Sodium 1258mg; Carbs 21. 87g; Fiber 0. 3g; Sugar 0. 73g; Protein 25. 21g

Turkey Sausage with Red Beans & Brown Rice

Prep time: 10 minutes | **Cook time:** 6-8 hours | **Serves:** 8

8 cups chicken stock (or store-bought) or fish stock	1 red bell pepper, seeded and chopped
1 pound dried red beans	1 sweet onion, chopped
1½ cups long-grain brown rice	3 garlic cloves, minced
½ teaspoon extra-virgin olive oil	2 tablespoons Creole seasoning
¾ pound smoked turkey sausage, cut into ½-inch slices	Finely chopped scallions and/or red onions, for garnish (optional)
3 celery stalks, chopped	
1 green bell pepper, seeded and chopped	

1. Place the stock, red beans, and rice in the pot. 2. Turn dial to Sear/Sauté, set temperature to LO, and press START/STOP to begin cooking. Heat the olive oil in the pot and add the sausage slices and sauté for about 4 minutes, turning once, until browned. 3. Add the celery, sweet onion, bell peppers, and garlic to the pot. Stir to mix well. Sprinkle in the Creole seasoning and stir, about 1 minute. Press START/STOP to turn off the Sear/Sauté function. 4. Cover with the lid and turn the dial to Slow Cook, cook on low for 6 to 8 hours, or until the beans and rice are tender. 5. Stir well. Serve garnished with the scallions and/or red onions, if desired.

Per Serving: Calories 342; Fat 8. 74g; Sodium 819mg; Carbs 48. 31g; Fiber 3. 4g; Sugar 7. 52g; Protein 17. 43g

Spiced Chicken with Sweet Potatoes

Prep time: 10 minutes | **Cook time:** 8 hours | **Serves:** 4

2 sweet potatoes, peeled and cubed	¼ teaspoon cayenne pepper
1 teaspoon garlic powder	¼ teaspoon freshly ground black pepper
1 teaspoon onion powder	¼ teaspoon ground nutmeg
1 teaspoon brown sugar	Pinch ground cinnamon
1 teaspoon sea salt	3 pounds chicken parts
½ teaspoon smoked paprika	3 tablespoons extra-virgin olive oil
½ teaspoon ground allspice	

1. Add the sweet potatoes to the pot. 2. In a small bowl, mix together the garlic powder, onion powder, brown sugar, salt, paprika, allspice, cayenne pepper, black pepper, nutmeg, and cinnamon. 3. Rub the spice mixture onto the chicken pieces. 4. Turn dial to Sear/Sauté, set temperature to LO, and press START/STOP to begin cooking. Heat the olive oil in the pot and add the chicken pieces, skin-side down, and cook for 4 to 6 minutes, or until the skin is browned. Press START/STOP to turn off the Sear/Sauté function. 5. Transfer the chicken to a bowl. Place the sweet potatoes in the bottom of the pot, spread the chicken on top, skin-side up. 6. Cover with the lid and turn the dial to Slow Cook, cook on low for 8 hours, or until the chicken reads 165°F on a food thermometer and the potatoes are tender.

Per Serving: Calories 486; Fat 13. 87g; Sodium 965mg; Carbs 15. 69g; Fiber 2. 5g; Sugar 3. 5g; Protein 70. 54g

Chapter 6 Beef, Pork and Lamb Recipes

Herbed Beef and Spaghetti

Prep time: 10 minutes | Cook time: 7-8 hours | Serves: 6

¾ pound 80% lean ground beef	¼ teaspoon dried red pepper flakes
1 onion, chopped	½ cup beef stock
3 cloves garlic, chopped	1 (26-ounce) jar pasta sauce
1 carrot, coarsely grated	1 (16-ounce) package spaghetti pasta
1 teaspoon dried basil leaves	⅓ cup grated Parmesan cheese

1. Turn dial to Sear/Sauté, set temperature to LO, and press START/STOP to begin cooking. Add the ground beef with onion and garlic to the pot, cook until beef is cooked, stirring to break up meat. 2. Add carrot, basil, red pepper flakes, stock, and pasta sauce to the pot. Cover with the lid and turn the dial to Slow Cook and cook on low for 7 to 8 hours, until sauce is bubbling and vegetables are tender. 3. Cook pasta according to package directions; drain, and serve with spaghetti sauce and meatballs. Top with Parmesan cheese.

Per Serving: Calories 314; Fat 10. 13g; Sodium 696mg; Carbs 33. 2g; Fiber 6. 2g; Sugar 8. 55g; Protein 23. 17g

Pork Chops with Apricot and Carrot

Prep time: 10 minutes | Cook time: 8 hours | Serves: 4

4 center-cut boneless pork chops	1 tablespoon Dijon mustard
½ cup dried apricots, chopped	3 tablespoons honey
½ cup apricot nectar	½ teaspoon salt
¼ cup apricot preserves	⅛ teaspoon white pepper
2 cloves garlic, minced	2 carrots, sliced

1. Place all ingredients in the pot, cover, and turn the dial to Slow Cook, cook on low for 8 hours or until pork chops and carrots are tender. 2. Serve with hot cooked rice, couscous, or pasta.

Per Serving: Calories 356; Fat 6. 9g; Sodium 442mg; Carbs 33. 68g; Fiber 2. 2g; Sugar 30. 41g; Protein 40. 39g

Swiss Steak and Carrot

Prep time: 10 minutes | Cook time: 8-10 hours | Serves: 6

1-pound round steak	2 cloves garlic, chopped
½ teaspoon salt	1 (8-ounce) can tomato sauce
⅛ teaspoon pepper	2 tablespoons olive oil
3 tablespoons flour	1 tablespoon Dijon mustard
3 carrots, sliced	½ teaspoon dried thyme leaves
1 onion, chopped	

1. First, slice the steak into pieces that are suitable for serving and place them on a sheet of waxed paper. Next, mix salt, pepper, and flour together in a small bowl and ensure they are well combined. 2. Sprinkle half of this mixture over the steak pieces, then use a meat mallet or rolling pin to press the flour mixture into the meat. Flip the meat over and repeat the same process on the other side using the remaining mixture. 3. Add the seasoned steak to the pot. Turn dial to Sear/Sauté, set temperature to LO, and press START/STOP to begin cooking. Cook for about 4 minutes' total. Add carrots, onions, and garlic and pour tomato sauce into the pot and bring to a boil, stirring to release any drippings. Press START/STOP to turn off the Sear/Sauté function. 4. Stir in mustard and thyme. Cover with the lid and turn the dial to Slow Cook. Cook on low for 8 to 10 hours, until meat and vegetables are very tender.

Per Serving: Calories 224; Fat 10. 6g; Sodium 302mg; Carbs 6. 85g; Fiber 1. 4g; Sugar 1. 96g; Protein 24. 28g

Sweet and Sour Pork Chops with Cabbage

Prep time: 10 minutes | Cook time: 7-8 hours | Serves: 4

1 onion, chopped	⅛ teaspoon white pepper
2 cloves garlic, minced	1 tablespoon olive oil
4 cups chopped green cabbage	¼ cup brown sugar
1 apple, chopped	¼ cup apple cider vinegar
4 (3. 5-ounce) boneless pork chops	1 tablespoon mustard

1. Mix together the onion, garlic, cabbage, and apple in a large bowl. 2. Trim pork chops of any excess fat and sprinkle with pepper. Turn dial to Sear/Sauté, set temperature to LO, and press START/STOP to begin cooking. Heat olive oil in the pot and brown chops on just one side, about 3 minutes. Add the vegetables. 3. Mix together the brown sugar, vinegar, and mustard in a bowl and mix well. Pour into the pot. Cover with the lid and turn the dial to Slow cook. Cook on low for 7–8 hours or until pork and cabbage are tender. Serve right away.

Per Serving: Calories 391; Fat 10. 11g; Sodium 164mg; Carbs 31. 42g; Fiber 3. 7g; Sugar 24. 18g; Protein 43. 43g

Pot Roast with Potato & Carrot

Prep time: 10 minutes | Cook time: 8-10 hours | Serves: 6

1 (1¼-pound) bottom round or chuck roast	1 onion, chopped
3 tablespoons all-purpose flour	2 potatoes, cubed
1 teaspoon salt	2 carrots, sliced
1 teaspoon paprika	1 (10-ounce) can condensed tomato soup
¼ teaspoon pepper	2 tablespoons cornstarch
1 tablespoon olive oil	⅓ cup water
1 tablespoon butter	

1. First, remove any extra fat from the roast. Then, mix flour, salt, paprika, and pepper on a flat plate. Coat the roast in this mixture. Next, heat a mixture of olive oil and butter in a big saucepan over medium heat. Add the roast and cook until brown on both sides, turning once, for around 5 to 8 minutes. 2. In the meantime, place the onions, potatoes, and carrots in the pot. Top with the browned roast. Pour ¼ cup water and tomato soup into saucepan and bring to a boil, scraping the pan to loosen drippings. Pour over roast. 3. Cover with the lid and turn the dial to Slow Cook, cook on low for 8–10 hours until meat and vegetables are very tender. If the gravy is too thin, you have the option to make it thicker. First, take out the roast and cover it with foil. 4. After that, mix cornstarch with half a cup of water in a small bowl and add it to the gravy. Cover the gravy and cook it on high heat for 20 to 30 minutes until it thickens.

Per Serving: Calories 304; Fat 8. 64g; Sodium 500mg; Carbs 30. 83g; Fiber 4. 3g; Sugar 3. 21g; Protein 25. 49g

Sweet & Sour Beef with Green Beans

Prep time: 10 minutes | Cook time: 8-10 hours | Serves: 4

1-pound bottom round steak, cubed	3 tablespoons sugar
3 tablespoons all-purpose flour	2 tablespoons low-sodium soy sauce
½ teaspoon salt	2 cups sliced carrots
⅛ teaspoon pepper	1 cup frozen green beans
1 onion, chopped	1 cup beef stock
1 (8-ounce) can pineapple tidbits	2 tablespoons cornstarch
¼ cup apple cider vinegar	

1. Toss cubed meat with flour, salt, and pepper. Add to the pot with onions. Drain pineapple, reserving liquid. Add pineapple, vinegar, sugar, and soy sauce to the pot; stir until blended. 2. Add carrots, green beans, and stock. Cover with the lid and turn the dial to Slow Cook, cook on low for 8–10 hours until beef is very tender. 3. Mix cornstarch with half a cup of the pineapple juice set aside in a small bowl. Pour the mixture into the pot, stir it, and cover it. 4. Cook on high for approximately 30 minutes or until the sauce thickens. Serve the sauce over hot cooked rice.

Per Serving: Calories 280; Fat 4. 75g; Sodium 740mg; Carbs 30. 38g; Fiber 2g; Sugar 17. 54g; Protein 28. 59g

Italian Sausage and Lasagna

Prep time: 10 minutes | **Cook time:** 6-8 hours | **Serves:** 5

¾ pound bulk Italian sausage	1 (3-ounce) package cream cheese, softened
1 onion, chopped	¾ cup part-skim ricotta cheese
3 cloves garlic, minced	1 egg
1 (8-ounce) can tomato sauce	1 cup shredded part-skim mozzarella cheese
¼ cup tomato paste	⅛ teaspoon pepper
1 teaspoon dried Italian seasoning	1 tablespoon dried parsley flakes
1 cup chicken stock	6 uncooked lasagna noodles

1. Cook the sausage in a large skillet until it is almost done, then remove any extra fat and add onion and garlic. 2. Continue cooking and stirring until the sausage is fully cooked and the vegetables are slightly crunchy. 3. Add tomato sauce, paste, Italian seasoning, and Stock. Simmer the sauce for 5 to 10 minutes, stirring often to mix the flavors. 4. While the sauce is cooking, mix cream cheese and ricotta cheese together in a large bowl until they are well combined. Add an egg and then stir in mozzarella cheese, pepper, and parsley. 5. Place ⅓ of the sauce in the bottom of the pot. Top with 2 lasagna noodles, breaking them as necessary to fit. 6. Top with ½ of the cheese mixture, then ⅓ of meat mixture. Top with 2 more lasagna noodles, then remaining cheese mixture. Finally, add remaining lasagna noodles and remaining meat mixture. 7. Cover and turn the dial to Slow Cook, cook on low for 6 to 8 hours until noodles are tender. 8. Serve by scooping up a large spoonful from the bottom of the pot.
Per Serving: Calories 635; Fat 31. 69g; Sodium 1060mg; Carbs 22. 93g; Fiber 3. 9g; Sugar 4. 94g; Protein 66. 26g

Cumin Pulled Pork

Prep time: 10 minutes | **Cook time:** 8-9 hours | **Serves:** 6

1½-pound pork roast	1 onion, chopped
½ teaspoon salt	3 cloves garlic, chopped
¼ teaspoon pepper	½ cup chicken stock
1 teaspoon cumin	

1. Rub the roast with salt, pepper, and cumin, and place in the pot. Surround with onions and garlic and pour chicken stock over all. 2. Cover with the lid and turn the dial to Slow Cook, cook on low for 8–9 hours until pork is very tender. Press START/STOP to turn off the Slow Cook function. 3. Remove pork from the pot. Place in a plate and shred the meat with 2 forks and place back to the pot. 4. Turn dial to Bake. Set the temperature to 400°F. Bake for 15–20 minutes or until pork is crisp on top. Stir pork mixture thoroughly and bake for 15–20 minutes longer or until pork is again crisp on top. 5. Serve with crisp tacos, flour or corn tortillas, and lots of salsa.
Per Serving: Calories 237; Fat 10. 35g; Sodium 276mg; Carbs 3. 25g; Fiber 0. 4g; Sugar 1. 21g; Protein 30. 9g

Juicy Pork Roast with Raisins

Prep time: 15 minutes | **Cook time:** 7–8 hours | **Serves:** 4

1 (1¼-pound) boneless pork shoulder roast	½ cup golden raisins
½ teaspoon salt	⅓ cup apple juice
¼ teaspoon pepper	3 tablespoons apple cider vinegar
3 tablespoons flour	2 tablespoons cornstarch
1 tablespoon butter	⅓ cup water
1 onion, chopped	½ cup chicken broth
2 cloves garlic, minced	½ teaspoon dried marjoram leaves
½ cup dark raisins	1 bay leaf

1. Cut roast into 2-inch pieces and sprinkle with salt, pepper, and flour. Add butter to the pot. Turn dial to Sear/Sauté, set temperature to LO, and press START/STOP to begin cooking. Once the butter is hot, add the pork to the pot. Brown the pork cubes about 2–3 minutes' total. 2. Add onion and garlic to the pot; cook and stir for 4–5 minutes to loosen pot drippings. Press START/STOP to turn off the Sear/Sauté function. Then, add all remaining ingredients except cornstarch and water to the pot. 3. Cover with the lid and turn the dial to Slow Cook, cook on low for 7–8 hours, or until pork registers 160°F. Remove bay leaf. 4. In small bowl combine cornstarch and water; stir into the pot and cook on high for 10–15 minutes until sauce is thickened. Serve over hot cooked rice.

Per Serving: Calories 386; Fat 10. 95g; Sodium 513mg; Carbs 30. 71g; Fiber 1. 7g; Sugar 15. 61g; Protein 40. 06g

Balsamic Beef with Red Cabbage

Prep time: 20 minutes | **Cook time:** 8 hours | **Serves:** 2

12 ounces beef stew meat, trimmed of excess fat and cut into 1-inch pieces	¼ cup balsamic vinegar
2 cups shredded red cabbage	1 teaspoon Dijon mustard
½ cup thinly sliced red onion	1 teaspoon ground cumin
¼ cup dry red wine	⅛ teaspoon sea salt
	Freshly ground black pepper

1. Put the beef in the pot and top with the cabbage and then the onions. 2. Add the wine, vinegar, mustard, cumin, salt, and a few grinds of the black pepper to a bowl and mix well. Pour this mixture into the pot. 3. Cover with the lid and turn the dial to Slow Cook, cook on low for 8 hours. Serve warm.

Per Serving: Calories 290; Fat 7. 28g; Sodium 357mg; Carbs 15. 82g; Fiber 2. 6g; Sugar 9. 44g; Protein 39. 31g

Red Wine–Braised Beef Brisket

Prep time: 20 minutes | **Cook time:** 8-10 hours | **Serves:** 2

16 ounces beef brisket, cut into two 8-ounce pieces
½ cup diced onion
1 teaspoon minced fresh rosemary
1 garlic clove, minced
¼ cup diced carrot
1 plum tomato, diced

1 cup low-sodium beef broth
½ cup dry red wine
1 tablespoon red wine vinegar
1 teaspoon tomato paste
¼ teaspoon sea salt

1. Add all the ingredients to the pot and stir well. 2. Cover with the lid and turn the dial to Slow Cook. Cook on low for 8 to 10 hours, or until the meat is very tender. 3. Transfer the brisket to a cutting board and shred it with a fork. Return it to the pot and stir it into the liquid to soak in even more flavor.

Per Serving: Calories 591; Fat 36. 81g; Sodium 1105mg; Carbs 22. 96g; Fiber 1. 5g; Sugar 8. 41g; Protein 39. 47g

Spiced Beef Roast with Mushrooms & Celery

Prep time: 20 minutes | **Cook time:** 8 hours | **Serves:** 2

1 teaspoon minced garlic
1 tablespoon tomato paste
¼ teaspoon ground allspice
⅛ teaspoon sea salt
Freshly ground black pepper
16 ounces beef chuck roast, trimmed of excess fat
2 carrots, cut into 2-inch pieces

1 celery stalk, cut into 2-inch pieces
2 shallots, peeled and halved
8 cremini mushrooms, halved
1 sprig fresh thyme
1 cup low-sodium beef broth
¼ cup dry red wine

1. Combine the garlic, tomato paste, salt, allspice, and a few grinds of the black pepper in a small bowl, stir to mix well. Rub the mixture all over the chuck roast, and then place it in the pot. 2. Add the carrots, mushrooms, celery, shallots, and thyme to the pot. Pour in the broth and wine. 3. Cover with the lid and turn the dial to Slow Cook. Cook on low for 8 hours.

Per Serving: Calories 558; Fat 22. 5g; Sodium 414mg; Carbs 22. 51g; Fiber 3. 3g; Sugar 5. 96g; Protein 69. 22g

Lemony Lamb Shoulder with Red Potatoes

Prep time: 20 minutes | **Cook time:** 8-10 hours | **Serves:** 2

4 garlic cloves, minced, divided	Freshly ground black pepper
Juice of 1 lemon	2 bone-in lamb shoulder chops, about 6 ounces each,
1 tablespoon minced fresh rosemary	trimmed of excess fat
1 tablespoon minced fresh oregano	4 red potatoes, halved
½ teaspoon ground cinnamon	Zest of 1 lemon
¼ teaspoon ground cumin	1 tablespoon extra-virgin olive oil
⅛ teaspoon sea salt	

1. Combine half of the garlic and the lemon juice, cinnamon, rosemary, oregano, cumin, salt, and a few grinds of the black pepper in a small bowl, stir to mix well. Rub the lamb chops with this mixture and set aside; you can do this the night before if you desired. 2. Place the potatoes, the remaining garlic, lemon zest, and olive oil in the pot a. Set the lamb shoulder on top. 3. Cover and turn the dial to Slow Cook, cook on low for 8 to 10 hours, until the lamb is tender and falling off the bone.

Per Serving: Calories 616; Fat 6. 91g; Sodium 374mg; Carbs 124. 16g; Fiber 13. 7g; Sugar 10. 85g; Protein 20. 57g

Curried Brown Rice with Ground Lamb

Prep time: 10 minutes | **Cook time:** 4-6 hours | **Serves:** 6

1 cup uncooked brown rice	2 teaspoons ground cumin
2 cups low-sodium chicken broth	2 teaspoons ground ginger
1 cup Marinara sauce	2 teaspoons ground turmeric
1 onion, chopped	1 teaspoon ground coriander
3 garlic cloves, minced	½ teaspoon ground cayenne pepper
2 teaspoons curry powder or garam masala	1-pound ground lamb, cooked

1. Add the rice, marinara sauce, onion, broth, garlic, curry powder, ginger, turmeric, cumin, coriander, and cayenne pepper to the pot. Stir to mix well. 2. Cover and turn the dial to Slow Cook, turn the dial to Slow Cook. Cook on low for 4 to 6 hours. 3. Stir in the ground lamb and serve.

Per Serving: Calories 307; Fat 11. 13g; Sodium 377mg; Carbs 32. 34g; Fiber 3g; Sugar 3. 15g; Protein 20. 76g

Beef Stew with Chopped Veggies & Olives

Prep time: 15 minutes | **Cook time:** 10 hours | **Serves:** 6

Cooking spray
3 pounds lean, boneless beef roast
4 cups beef stock
4 celery ribs, chopped
3 poblano chiles, diced
2 red bell peppers, diced
2 carrots, chopped
1 onion, chopped

1 habanero chile, left whole
1 bay leaf
4 garlic cloves, crushed
2 large tomatoes, diced
1 teaspoon dried Mexican oregano
1 teaspoon ground cumin
1 teaspoon sea salt
½ cup sliced Spanish olives

1. Spray the pot with cooking spray. 2. Add all the ingredients to the pot except the olives, stir well. Cover and turn the dial to Slow Cook, cook on low for 10 hours or on high for 5 hours. 3. Discard the habanero. 4. Transfer the beef to a cutting board and shred it using two forks. Then, return the shredded beef to the pot and stir it into the broth. 5. Spread the olives on top and serve.

Per Serving: Calories 781; Fat 31. 17g; Sodium 1345mg; Carbs 90. 68g; Fiber 8. 8g; Sugar 27. 42g; Protein 36. 63g

Green Salsa Braised Beef & Pork

Prep time: 15 minutes | **Cook time:** 18 hours | **Serves:** 6

Cooking spray
1½ pounds lean, boneless beef roast
1½ pounds lean, boneless pork roast
2 tablespoons Fajita seasoning mix

1 cup green salsa or 1 (14. 5-ounce) can green
enchilada sauce
2 poblano chiles, fire-roasted, peeled, seeded, and diced

The Night Before: 1. Spray the pot with cooking spray. 2. Rub the beef and pork with fajita seasoning. 3. Place the meat in the pot, cover and turn the dial to Slow Cook. Cook on low for 10 hours

In the Morning: 1. Transfer the meat to a cutting board and drain the liquid from the pot (save it for sauces and stocks). Shred the meat using two forks. 2. Place the shredded meat in the pot, spread the Green Salsa and poblanos on top, and cook on Slow Cook function for 8 hours on low. 3. Use the meat in tostadas, enchiladas, tacos, burritos, or tortas.

Per Serving: Calories 613; Fat 20. 7g; Sodium 1543mg; Carbs 79. 28g; Fiber 5. 6g; Sugar 21. 05g; Protein 27. 43g

Spiced Pork Loin with Cabbage Slaw

Prep time: 15 minutes | Cook time: 8 hours | Serves: 4

1 tsp. of nutmeg	2 white of onions, chopped
1 tsp. of allspice	2 cups of water
1 tbsp. of dried sage	2 carrots, peeled and grated
1 tbsp. of olive oil	1 cup of white cabbage, washed and grated or spiralized
8 oz. of lean pork loin	1 lime, juiced
1 tsp. of cloves	

1. In a small bowl, combine the nutmeg, allspice, sage and olive oil, stir to mix well. 2. Coat the pork with this mixture. 3. When ready to cook, evenly press the cloves into the pork. 4. Add the pork loin with the onions and water to the pot. 5. Cover and turn the dial to Slow Cook, cook on low for 8 hours until the pork is very soft. 6. In the meantime, prepare the slaw. 7. Mix together the carrot and cabbage in a bowl, and squeeze over the lime juice. 8. Cover and place in the fridge until you're ready to serve. 9. Remove the loin from the pot and slice generously. 10. Serve with the slaw, onions and a drizzle of the juices. 11. Pick out the cloves before serving!

Per Serving: Calories 223; Fat 9. 26g; Sodium 69mg; Carbs 17. 89g; Fiber 3. 1g; Sugar 10. 16g; Protein 17. 73g

Pork Chops with Orange Mashed Sweet Potatoes

Prep time: 15 minutes | Cook time: 6-8 hours | Serves: 4

3 large sweet potatoes, peeled and diced	4 bone-in pork chops, about 8 ounces each
Grated zest of 1 orange	Sea salt
Pinch ground nutmeg	Freshly ground black pepper
½ cup chicken stock	3 tablespoons unsalted butter, at room temperature

1. Add the sweet potatoes, orange zest, nutmeg, and stock to the pot. Gently stir them well. 2. Season the pork chops with salt and black pepper. Then arrange them on top of the sweet potatoes. 3. Cover with the lid and turn the dial to Slow Cook, cook on low for 6 to 8 hours, until the sweet potatoes are completely soft and the pork is cooked to at least 145°F on a food thermometer. 4. Take out the pork chops from the cooking pot and transfer them onto a fresh plate, then cover them up. 5. Mix in some butter with the sweet potatoes that are still in the pot, and use either a potato masher or the back of a spoon to mash them up. 6. Serve the mashed sweet potatoes alongside the pork chops.

Per Serving: Calories 246; Fat 9. 52g; Sodium 256mg; Carbs 29. 55g; Fiber 4. 5g; Sugar 9. 55g; Protein 11. 12g

Sweet & Sour Country-Style Pork Ribs

Prep time: 15 minutes | Cook time: 8 hours | Serves: 6

3 pounds country-style spareribs
1 cup unsweetened pineapple juice
2 tablespoons low-sodium soy sauce
¼ cup apple cider vinegar
1 tablespoon chili garlic sauce
1 teaspoon grated orange zest

1 tablespoon cornstarch
1 teaspoon fish sauce
1 teaspoon garlic powder
1 teaspoon onion powder
½ teaspoon sea salt

1. Place the spareribs in the pot. 2. Combine the pineapple juice, chili, soy sauce, vinegar, orange zest, garlic sauce, fish sauce, cornstarch, garlic powder, onion powder, and salt in a medium bowl and stir well to mix. 3. Pour the sauce over the pork. 4. Cover with the lid and turn the dial to Slow Cook, cook on low for 8 hours, or until the meat is very tender.

Per Serving: Calories 355; Fat 13. 44g; Sodium 668mg; Carbs 10. 56g; Fiber 0. 7g; Sugar 7. 46g; Protein 48. 73g

Spanish-Style Lamb Chops with Red Potatoes

Prep time: 15 minutes | Cook time: 8 hours | Serves: 2

1 teaspoon extra-virgin olive oil
½ cup diced onion
½ cup diced roasted red pepper
2 tablespoons fresh parsley
½ cup red wine
⅛ teaspoon sea salt

Freshly ground black pepper
1 teaspoon minced garlic
½ teaspoon minced fresh rosemary
1 teaspoon smoked paprika
2 bone-in lamb shoulders, trimmed of fat
2 red potatoes, unpeeled, quartered

1. Grease the pot with the olive oil. 2. Add the onion, red pepper, parsley, and wine to the pot. 3. Mix together the salt, a few grinds of the black pepper, rosemary, garlic, and paprika in a small bowl. Rub this mixture over the lamb chops. 4. To enhance the taste of the dish, it is recommended to prepare the meat a day before so that the seasoning can fully penetrate the meat. 5. Then, put the meat on the onion and wine mixture in the pot. It's okay if the meat slightly overlaps to fit. Place the potatoes on top of the lamb. 6. Cover with the lid and turn the dial to Slow Cook, cook on low for 8 hours. Serve warm.

Per Serving: Calories 483; Fat 11. 31g; Sodium 334mg; Carbs 65. 14g; Fiber 7. 8g; Sugar 7. 63g; Protein 30. 68g

Lime Pork with Chimichurri

Prep time: 15 minutes | Cook time: 8-10 hours | Serves: 6-8

1 bunch fresh parsley	2 tablespoons apple cider vinegar
1 bunch fresh cilantro	½ cup extra-virgin olive oil, plus 1 tablespoon
1 tablespoon dried oregano	1 teaspoon sea salt
4 garlic cloves, peeled	1 teaspoon freshly ground black pepper
Zest and juice of 1 lime	1 (2½- to 3-pound) pork butt (also called pork shoulder)

1. Add the parsley, cilantro, vinegar, garlic, oregano, lime zest and juice, ½ cup of olive oil, salt, and black pepper to a blender, and blend until mostly smooth. Set aside. 2. Coat the inside of the pot with the remaining 1 tablespoon of oil. 3. Put the pork butt in the pot. Pour about half of the chimichurri sauce over the pork. Refrigerate the remaining chimichurri. 4. Cover with the lid and turn the dial to Slow Cook, cook on low for 8 to 10 hours, or until the meat is cooked to an internal temperature of 145°F. 5. Let the meat rest for 15 minutes, then cut it into slices and serve with the remaining chimichurri on the side.

Per Serving: Calories 314; Fat 13. 29g; Sodium mg; Carbs 1. 74g; Fiber 0. 4g; Sugar 0. 18g; Protein 44. 1g

Balsamic Pork Tenderloin with Peach Sauce

Prep time: 15 minutes | Cook time: 5-6 hours | Serves: 6

1 tablespoon canola oil	½ cup low-sodium chicken broth, or store-bought
4 cups peeled sliced peaches	2 (1½-pound) pork tenderloins
1 tablespoon minced fresh rosemary	Sea salt
1 medium red onion, halved and thinly sliced	Freshly ground black pepper
1 garlic clove, peeled and smashed	2 tablespoons brown sugar
¼ cup balsamic vinegar	

1. Coat the inside of the pot with the oil, making sure to cover about two-thirds up the sides of the pot. 2. Place the peaches, onion, rosemary, and garlic in the pot. Pour in the vinegar and chicken broth. 3. Place the pork on top of the peach mixture and season with salt and black pepper. 4. Cover with the lid and turn the dial to Slow Cook, cook on low for 5 to 6 hours, until the meat is cooked to an internal temperature of 145°F. 5. Remove it from the pot and transfer it to a cutting board. Let the meat rest for 15 minutes before cutting it into slices. 6. Mix the brown sugar with the peach sauce, raise the heat to high, and let it boil without covering until the liquid reduces and the sauce becomes thick and sticky, which usually takes around 15 minutes. 7. Serve the pork with the sauce.

Per Serving: Calories 413; Fat 8. 49g; Sodium 211mg; Carbs 39. 94g; Fiber 2. 4g; Sugar 36. 85g; Protein 44. 87g

Smoky Pork Stew with White Hominy

Prep time: 15 minutes | **Cook time:** 10 hours | **Serves:** 6

1 teaspoon smoked salt	6 garlic cloves
½ teaspoon freshly ground black pepper	4 to 6 jalapeños, seeded and sliced
½ teaspoon smoked paprika	4 bottles Mexican beer, such as Corona, Sol, or Negra
3 pounds lean, boneless pork roast	Modelo
2 tablespoons olive oil	¾ cup chopped fresh cilantro
1 large onion, chopped	1½ teaspoons dried Mexican oregano
2 cups Green Salsa	2 (15. 5-ounce) cans white hominy, rinsed and drained

The Night Before: 1. Add the salt, pepper, and smoked paprika to a small bowl, stir to mix well. Rub this spice mixture over the meat to cover it completely. 2. Add the olive oil to the pot. Turn dial to Sear/Sauté, set temperature to LO, and press START/STOP to begin cooking. When the oil is hot and just beginning to smoke, add the meat to the pot and sear it on all sides. Transfer the meat to a storage container, leave it uncovered. 3. Add the onions to the pot; sauté for 1 minute until they begin to soften. Remove the cooked onions to the storage container with the beef. When the ingredients have cooled, seal the container and place it in the refrigerator.

In the Morning: 1. Add the meat and onions, the jalapeños, the garlic, and the beer to the pot, stir well. Cover and turn the dial to Slow Cook, cook on low for 10 hours or on high for 5½ hours. 2. Stir in the cilantro, oregano, and hominy, and cook for another 15 minutes just to heat the hominy. 3. Serve with a little diced avocado and grated cheese on top, if desired.

Per Serving: Calories 723; Fat 24. 12g; Sodium 1638mg; Carbs 100. 91g; Fiber 10g; Sugar 28. 02g; Protein 27. 89g

Chapter 7 Fish and Seafood Recipes

Creamy Red Snapper Fillets with Beans & Corn

Prep time: 15 minutes | Cook time: 8-9 hours | Serves: 4

1 onion, chopped	¼ cup apple cider vinegar
1 (10-ounce) package frozen lima beans	¼ cup sugar
2 stalks celery, chopped	2 tablespoons butter
2 cups frozen corn kernels	⅓ cup sour cream
½ teaspoon salt	½ pound red snapper fillets Salt and pepper to taste
½ teaspoon ground ginger	½ teaspoon paprika
⅛ teaspoon pepper	

1. Combine together the onions, lima beans, corn, ginger, celery, salt, and pepper in the pot, mix gently. In a small bowl, mix together vinegar and sugar; blend well. Pour into pot. 2. Cover with the lid and turn the dial to Slow Cook, cook on low for 7–8 hours or until succotash is blended and hot. Stir in butter and sour cream. 3. Season the fillets with salt, pepper, and paprika as desired. Take some of the succotash from the pot and place it on top of the fillets. Layer the fish and succotash in the pot, ensuring that the fillets are not touching each other. 4. Cover the pot and cook on low heat for 1 to 1½ hours, or until the fish is flaky when tested with a fork. 5. After cooking, stir the mixture to blend the fish and succotash, and serve immediately.
Per Serving: Calories 305; Fat 9. 22g; Sodium 395mg; Carbs 49. 11g; Fiber 6. 6g; Sugar 14. 3g; Protein 8. 77g

Rosemary Fish Fillets with Tomatoes

Prep time: 15 minutes | Cook time: 25 minutes | Serves: 2

2 firm white fish fillets, each weighing 6oz	½ tsp brown sugar
1 garlic clove, crushed	1 tbsp low fat mayonnaise
4 vine ripened tomatoes, sliced	Salt & pepper to taste
1 tsp freshly chopped rosemary	

1. In a bowl, mix together the garlic, rosemary sliced tomatoes, and sugar. Stir in the fish and toss well to coat. Place the fish in the bottom of the pot and top with the tomato mixture. 2. Cover and turn the dial to Bake. Cook at 380°F for 20-25 minutes or until the fish is cooked through and the tomatoes are tender. 3. Transfer the fish and tomatoes to a plate, serve with a dollop of low fat mayo.
Per Serving: Calories 251; Fat 12. 45g; Sodium 176mg; Carbs 12g; Fiber 2. 4g; Sugar 2. 57g; Protein 23. 85g

Fish Burritos

Prep time: 15 minutes | **Cook time:** 7-8 hours | **Serves:** 4

1 tablespoon olive oil	24 frozen fish fingers
1 onion, chopped	1 tablespoon chili powder
1 green bell pepper, chopped	½ cup Suave Cooked Salsa
1 (15-ounce) can black beans, drained	1 cup shredded Monterey jack cheese
1 (4-ounce) can green chiles, drained	4 (10-inch) flour tortillas

1. Add olive oil to the pot. Turn dial to Sear/Sauté, set temperature to LO, and press START/STOP to begin cooking. Once the oil is hot, add the onion; cook and stir for 3 minutes. Press START/STOP to turn off the Sear/Sauté function. Add bell pepper, beans, and chiles. 2. Cover with the lid and turn the dial to Slow Cook, cook on low for 6–7 hours or until vegetables are tender. Transfer to a bowl. 3. Clean and dry the pot. Place the fish fingers inside. Arrange in single layer. Turn the dial to Bake and set the temperature to 400°F. Bake for about 15 minutes. 4. When fish is done, remove from the pot. Spoon the bean mixture on tortillas, put fish on top, then wrap up, folding in ends. 5. Place the wraps in the pot, seam side down. Bake for 15–25 minutes or until tortillas start to brown and cheese is melted. Cut each in half and serve right away.

Per Serving: Calories 806; Fat 44. 2g; Sodium 1577mg; Carbs 71. 29g; Fiber 7. 5g; Sugar 8. 23g; Protein 32. 8g

Balsamic Tuna Steaks with Rice

Prep time: 15 minutes | **Cook time:** 5-6 hours | **Serves:** 2

3½oz long grain rice	1 garlic clove, crushed
1 cup hot vegetable stock	2 tbsp soy sauce
2 fresh tuna steaks, each weighing 5oz	Salt & pepper to taste
3 tbsp balsamic vinegar	

1. Add the rice and stock to the pot. Cover and turn the dial to Slow Cook. Cook on high for 4 hours. 2. Meanwhile, mix together the balsamic vinegar, garlic & soy sauce in a large bowl, stir in the tuna steaks. Place in the fridge and chill for 2-4 hours. 3. Once the rice is cooked, spread the marinated tuna on top. Cover and cook on low for 1-2 hours or until the tuna is cooked through and the rice is tender. 4. Serve the tuna steaks on a bed of rice.

Per Serving: Calories 384; Fat 5. 75g; Sodium 602mg; Carbs 48. 99g; Fiber 2. 4g; Sugar 8. 24g; Protein 33. 29g

Shrimp with Creamy Grits

Prep time: 15 minutes | **Cook time:** 8-9 hours | **Serves:** 4

2½ cups water	3 slices bacon
1½ cups milk	1 green bell pepper, chopped
1 cup quick-cooking grits	2 cloves garlic, minced
½ teaspoon salt	1 (8-ounce) can tomato sauce
½ teaspoon hot sauce	2 teaspoons chili powder
1 onion, chopped	8 ounces frozen cooked small shrimp, thawed
2 tablespoons butter	2 tablespoons cornstarch
1 cup grated sharp Cheddar cheese	3 tablespoons water

1. Add the water, milk, grits, hot sauce, salt, butter, and onions to the pot. Cover and turn the dial to Slow Cook. Cook on low for 8–9 hours or until grits are thick and creamy. Stir in cheese. 2. In a large saucepan, cook the bacon until crisp. Remove bacon, crumble, and set aside. 3. Add garlic and bell pepper to the drippings in the skillet and cook until they become crisp-tender which takes about 4 minutes. 4. Then, mix tomato sauce and chili powder in a saucepan and bring it to a simmer. After that, add shrimp and stir it. 5. Mix water and cornstarch in a small bowl and stir it into the saucepan. Keep stirring until it becomes thickened. 6. Put grits in a serving dish and add the shrimp mixture on top. 7. Sprinkle some reserved bacon on it and serve immediately.

Per Serving: Calories 470; Fat 30. 5g; Sodium 936mg; Carbs 34. 95g; Fiber 2. 7g; Sugar 19. 6g; Protein 15. 87g

Gingered Fish Fillets with Broccoli

Prep time: 10 minutes | **Cook time:** 15 minutes | **Serves:** 2

2 firm white fish fillets, each weighing 6oz	2 tbsp soy sauce
1 tsp freshly grated ginger	9 oz. tender stem broccoli
1 garlic clove, crushed	Salt & pepper to taste
2 tbsp oyster sauce	

1. In a medium bowl, mix together the garlic, ginger, oyster and soy sauces to form a marinade. 2. Place the fish fillets side by side in the pot and brush with a little of the marinade. 3. Add the broccoli to the remainder of the marinade in the bowl and combine well. Spread the broccoli over the fish. 4. Cover with the lid and Bake at 400°F for about 15 minutes or until the fish is cooked through and the broccoli is tender. 5. Transfer to a plate, season and serve.

Per Serving: Calories 279; Fat 14. 22g; Sodium 850mg; Carbs 12. 37g; Fiber 4. 2g; Sugar 4. 74g; Protein 26. 68g

Shrimp with Black Beans & Rice

Prep time: 15 minutes | **Cook time:** 8-9 hours | **Serves:** 4

2 cups dried black beans	3 cups water
1 tablespoon olive oil	1 (14-ounce) can diced tomatoes, undrained
1 cup brown rice	½ teaspoon cumin
1 onion, chopped	½ teaspoon salt
3 garlic cloves, minced	⅛ teaspoon cayenne pepper
2 cups vegetable broth	8 ounces frozen tiny cooked shrimp, thawed

1. To prepare this dish, on the evening before you plan to serve it, separate the beans and wash them thoroughly. Then, cover the beans with cold water and let them soak overnight. The next morning, drain the water and rinse the beans again. 2. Add the olive oil to the pot. Turn dial to Sear/Sauté, set temperature to LO, and press START/STOP to begin cooking. 3. Once the oil is hot, add rice, onion, and garlic; cook and stir for 3–5 minutes or until fragrant. Press START/STOP to turn off the Sear/Sauté function. 4. Add the beans, garlic, onion, vegetable broth, and water. Cover with the lid and turn the dial to Slow Cook. Cook on low for 6 hours, stirring every two hours. 5. Then add the tomatoes, cumin, salt, and pepper, stirring well. Cover and cook on low for 2–3 hours longer until rice and beans are tender. 6. Stir in shrimp, cover, and cook for 20 minutes more, then serve.

Per Serving: Calories 623; Fat 7. 79g; Sodium 581mg; Carbs 110. 69g; Fiber 19. 9g; Sugar 7. 32g; Protein 30. 22g

Creamy Orange Fish with Sweet Potatoes

Prep time: 15 minutes | **Cook time:** 8-9 hours | **Serves:** 4

3 sweet potatoes, peeled	½ teaspoon salt
1 onion, chopped	⅛ teaspoon pepper
3 cloves garlic, minced	½ pound fish fillets
1 tablespoon minced gingerroot	½ cup sour cream
¼ cup brown sugar	2 tablespoons orange marmalade
¼ cup orange juice	2 tablespoons orange juice concentrate, thawed
1 tablespoon butter	¼ teaspoon ground ginger

1. Cut sweet potatoes into 1-inch cubes and place in the pot, along with onions, garlic, and gingerroot. Mix together the brown sugar, butter, orange juice, salt, and pepper in a small bowl. Spoon over potatoes. 2. Cover with the lid and turn the dial to Slow Cook. Cook on low for 7–8 hours or until potatoes are tender when pierced with fork. 3. Put the fish fillets over the potatoes. Cover and cook on low heat for 1 to 1½ hours, or until the fish can be easily flaked with a fork. Mix everything together. 4. While waiting, mix sour cream, thawed concentrate, marmalade, and ground ginger in a small bowl. Mix them well. Serve the mixture together with the fish and potatoes.

Per Serving: Calories 291; Fat 13. 12g; Sodium 647mg; Carbs 34. 87g; Fiber 2. 4g; Sugar 17. 29g; Protein 10. 74g

Lemony Salmon & Watercress Rice

Prep time: 15 minutes | **Cook time:** 5 hours | **Serves:** 2

3½ oz. long grain rice	2 tsp lemon juice
1 cup boiling water	2 tbsp white wine
Large pinch of salt	Large handful fresh watercress, chopped
2 boneless salmon fillets, each weighing 5oz	Salt & pepper to taste

1. Add the rice, water & salt to the pot. Cover and turn the dial to Slow Cook. Cook on high for 4 hours. 2. Meanwhile, place the salmon fillets and all the remaining ingredients in a bowl, stir well. Marinate for 2-4 hours in the fridge. 3. Once the rice is cooked, place the marinated salmon on top of the rice, cook on Slow Cook function on high heat for 1 hour or until the fish is cooked through and the rice is tender. 4. When the rice is cooked, Arrange the fillets on a plate. Fluff the rice up with a fork and quickly combine with the chopped watercress. 5. Serve the salmon with the rice on the side.

Per Serving: Calories 383; Fat 7. 28g; Sodium 317mg; Carbs 41. 17g; Fiber 2. 2g; Sugar 1. 89g; Protein 36. 61g

Lemon Shrimp and Artichoke Sorghum Risotto

Prep time: 15 minutes | **Cook time:** 3-4 hours | **Serves:** 4

1 tablespoon extra-virgin olive oil	1 (12-ounce) package frozen quartered artichoke hearts
1 cup chopped yellow onion	½ teaspoon freshly ground black pepper
4 garlic cloves, minced	1-pound large shrimp, peeled and deveined (uncooked,
1 red bell pepper, chopped	thawed if frozen)
¼ cup freshly squeezed lemon juice	2 ounces Pecorino-Romano cheese, grated
1 cup whole grain sorghum, rinsed	4 ounces baby spinach
3 cups low-sodium chicken broth	⅓ cup chopped fresh parsley
¼ cup chopped sun-dried tomatoes, not packed in oil	

1. Heat the olive oil to the pot. Turn dial to Sear/Sauté, set temperature to LO, and press START/STOP to begin cooking. Once the oil is hot, add the onion and sauté until translucent, about 5 minutes. 2. Add the garlic and bell pepper and cook for 1 more minute. 3. Add the lemon juice, increase the heat to HI, and cook until liquid is absorbed, about 1 minute. 4. Press START/STOP to turn off the Sear/Sauté function. Stir in the sorghum, sun-dried tomatoes, artichokes, broth, and black pepper. 5. Cover and turn the dial to Slow Cook. Cook on high for 3 to 4 hours, until sorghum is tender and the liquid is almost absorbed. 6. Around 15 minutes prior to serving, mix in the shrimp and cheese, then cover and keep cooking on high for 10 more minutes, or until the shrimp become opaque. 7. Add the baby spinach and stir until it becomes wilted, then include the parsley and divide the mixture evenly among serving bowls. The dish should be served right away.

Per Serving: Calories 377; Fat 11. 62g; Sodium 1008mg; Carbs 41. 45g; Fiber 7. 2g; Sugar 4. 32g; Protein 30. 44g

Seafood and Vegetables Stew

Prep time: 15 minutes | **Cook time:** 4-5 hours | **Serves:** 6

2 cups chopped onion
2 medium stalks celery, finely chopped
4 ounces frozen spinach
5 garlic cloves, minced
1 (28-ounce) can no-salt-added diced tomatoes, undrained
½ cup low-sodium vegetable broth
1 tablespoon red wine vinegar
1 tablespoon extra-virgin olive oil

3 teaspoons no-salt lemon pepper seasoning
¼ teaspoon sugar
¼ teaspoon crushed red pepper flakes
¼ cup chopped fresh parsley
1-pound cod fillets, cut into 1-inch pieces
¼ pound uncooked medium shrimp, shells and tails removed
¼ pound scallops
¼ pound crab meat

1. Add the onion, celery, tomatoes, spinach, garlic, olive oil, lemon pepper seasoning, red pepper flakes, sugar, broth, vinegar, and parsley to the pot, stir well. Cover and turn the dial to Slow Cook. cook on high for 4 hours. 2. Add the cod, scallops, shrimp, and crab. Cover and cook for an additional 30 to 45 minutes or until the fish is opaque and flakes with a fork. 3. Serve warm.

Per Serving: Calories 369; Fat 16. 07g; Sodium 621mg; Carbs 26. 37g; Fiber 12. 2g; Sugar 6. 85g; Protein 32. 19g

Lemony Tilapia with Asparagus & Peppers

Prep time: 15 minutes | **Cook time:** 20 minutes | **Serves:** 6

4 (6- to 8-ounce) tilapia fillets
4 teaspoons lemon pepper, divided
½ cup freshly squeezed lemon juice, divided

4 teaspoons butter, divided
1-pound asparagus, trimmed
1 red bell pepper, sliced

1. Cut 4 large pieces of foil, big enough to make fillet packets. 2. Lay each fillet evenly in the pot and sprinkle each with 1 teaspoon lemon pepper and 2 tablespoons lemon juice. Top each with 1 teaspoon butter. 3. Top each packet with one-quarter of the asparagus and one-quarter of the bell pepper. 4. Cover and turn the dial to Bake. Bake at 380°F for 20 minutes. Serve immediately.

Per Serving: Calories 131; Fat 4. 1g; Sodium 65mg; Carbs 7. 84g; Fiber 2. 2g; Sugar 3. 86g; Protein 18. 03g

Baked Mahi–Mahi with Pineapple Salsa

Prep time: 15 minutes | **Cook time:** 8 minutes | **Serves:** 4

½ cup medium diced fresh pineapple, grilled or un-grilled

¼ cup thinly sliced red onion

½ jalapeño, minced

1½ teaspoons coarsely chopped fresh cilantro

1½ teaspoons coarsely chopped fresh mint

1 tablespoon rice wine vinegar

1 tablespoon freshly squeezed lime juice

2 tablespoons extra-virgin olive oil, plus 1 teaspoon

4 (6-ounce) mahi-mahi fillets

Freshly ground black pepper

1. Turn dial to Bake, set temperature to 370°F, set time to 5 minutes and press START/STOP to begin preheating. 2. To make the relish, Mix together the pineapple, cilantro, mint, red onion, jalapeño, lime juice, vinegar, and 1 teaspoon of the olive oil in a bowl. 3. Coat the mahi-mahi fillets on both sides with the remaining 2 tablespoons olive oil and season with black pepper. Transfer to the preheated pot. 4. Bake for about 4 minutes per side. Serve with the pineapple salsa.

Per Serving: Calories 404; Fat 22. 83g; Sodium 470mg; Carbs 14. 07g; Fiber 5. 7g; Sugar 5. 83g; Protein 34. 98g

Cod and Squash with Tomato–Thyme Salsa

Prep time: 15 minutes | **Cook time:** 15 minutes | **Serves:** 4

Cooking spray

2 medium tomatoes, diced

3 tablespoons chopped fresh thyme

2 teaspoons chopped fresh oregano

1 tablespoon minced garlic

2 teaspoons extra-virgin olive oil

4 (4- to 6-ounce) cod fillets

2 cups sliced summer squash

Freshly ground black pepper

1. Lightly coat the inside of the pot with cooking spray. Turn dial to Bake, set temperature to 350°F, set time to 5 minutes and press START/STOP to begin preheating. 2. Mix together the tomato, oregano, thyme, and garlic in a small bowl. Add the olive oil and stir well. 3. Arrange the cod filets and squash slices in the pot. Spread the tomato mixture over the fish. Lightly spray the squash with cooking spray and season with ground black pepper. 4. Bake until the fish is opaque throughout when tested with the tip of a knife, 10 to 15 minutes. 5. Transfer one filet and ¼ of the squash to each of 4 serving plates and serve right away.

Per Serving: Calories 273; Fat 16. 46g; Sodium 440mg; Carbs 11. 7g; Fiber 6. 5g; Sugar 2. 39g; Protein 20. 41g

Cabbage–Stuffed Flounder Rolls

Prep time: 15 minutes | **Cook time:** 15 minutes | **Serves:** 4

Cooking spray
2 teaspoons extra-virgin olive oil
4 cups shredded cabbage
½ cup sliced mushrooms

1 tablespoon minced garlic
Freshly ground black pepper
4 (5- to 6-ounce) flounder (sole) fillets
1 teaspoon butter

1. Lightly coat a baking dish with cooking spray. Turn dial to Bake, set temperature to 400°F, set time to 5 minutes and press START/STOP to begin preheating. 2. Heat olive oil in a medium-sized skillet over medium heat. Put in the cabbage, garlic, mushrooms, and black pepper and cook by stirring until the cabbage starts to soften, for about 2-3 minutes. 3. Place the flounder fillets in the preheated pot. Place ¼ of the cabbage mixture in the middle of each fillet and roll up. Arrange the rolled fillets seam-side down in the pot. Brush with melted butter. 4. Bake until the fish is opaque throughout when tested with the tip of a knife, 8 to 10 minutes. 5. Transfer to individual plates and serve immediately.

Per Serving: Calories 295; Fat 17. 38g; Sodium 468mg; Carbs 14. 98g; Fiber 7. 1g; Sugar 4. 13g; Protein 21. 01g

Chapter 8 Dessert Recipes

Curried Fruit Granola

Prep time: 15 minutes | Cook time: 5-7 hours | Serves: 8

1 cup chopped dates
1 cup chopped prunes
1 (15-ounce) can apricots, chopped
1 (8-ounce) can pineapple tidbits, drained

½ cup brown sugar
2 teaspoons curry powder
2 cups granola

1. Combine all ingredients except granola in the pot. Cover and turn the dial to Slow Cook, cook on low for 4–5 hours or until sugar dissolves. 2. Add granola and cook it on high heat without covering it for 1-2 hours or until the mixture becomes thick. 3. Serve it with ice cream or whipped cream.

Per Serving: Calories 568; Fat 1. 08g; Sodium 22mg; Carbs 141. 37g; Fiber 3. 5g; Sugar 120. 16g; Protein 4. 24g

Red Wine–Poached Pears

Prep time: 15 minutes | Cook time: 7-9 hours | Serves: 6

2½ cups dry red wine
½ cup orange juice
1 cup sugar

4 large pears
1 cinnamon stick
¼ teaspoon salt

1. Mix together the wine, sugar, orange juice, cinnamon stick, and salt in the pot. Cover and turn the dial to Slow Cook, cook on low for 2–3 hours or until sugar dissolves. 2. Cut pears in half and take out the core, while keeping the stem attached to one half. Add the pears to a mixture of wine, cover, and cook on low heat for 5-6 hours, making sure to spoon the sauce over the pears twice during the cooking time. 3. Once the pears are cooked, remove the cinnamon stick and the pears from the mixture. 4. Put the cooked pears on a serving dish and pour 1 cup of the wine mixture over them. Allow them to cool before serving.

Per Serving: Calories 185; Fat 0. 26g; Sodium 107mg; Carbs 43. 69g; Fiber 5. 5g; Sugar 33g; Protein 0. 78g

Caramel Cream Marshmallow Fondue

Prep time: 15 minutes | **Cook time:** 3-4 hours | **Serves:** 8

1 (14-ounce) package caramels	1 cup miniature marshmallows
½ cup cream	1 tablespoon rum, if desired

1. Unwrap caramels and combine with cream in the pot. Cover with the lid and turn the dial to Slow Cook. Cook on low for 2–3 hours, stirring twice during cooking time, until the caramels are melted. 2. Mix in marshmallows and rum (if desired), then cover and cook on low heat for an additional hour, stirring twice during the cooking process, until the mixture is creamy. 3. Serve immediately.

Per Serving: Calories 283; Fat 15. 53g; Sodium 89mg; Carbs 32. 4g; Fiber 1. 2g; Sugar 22. 77g; Protein 3. 69g

Fruit Bread Pudding

Prep time: 15 minutes | **Cook time:** 3-4 hours | **Serves:** 6

1 (15-ounce) can fruit cocktail	½ cup light cream
1 (15-ounce) can sliced peaches	1 teaspoon vanilla
1½ cups sugar	½ teaspoon salt
3 eggs	8 slices white bread
½ cup butter, melted	

1. First, strain the fruit cocktail and peaches, but keep ¼ cup of juice from the peaches. Then, put them together in a big bowl and use a potato masher to crush some of the fruit. 2. Next, mix in sugar, eggs, cream, butter, vanilla, and salt until well combined. Finally, transfer the mixture into a pot. 3. Toast the bread and crumble. Stir into fruit mixture. Cover and turn the dial to Slow Cook. Cook on high for 3–4 hours until pudding is set.

Per Serving: Calories 609; Fat 24. 92g; Sodium 563mg; Carbs 89. 02g; Fiber 5g; Sugar 43. 2g; Protein 9. 75g

Tasty Chocolate Coconut Peanut Clusters

Prep time: 15 minutes | Cook time: 3-4 hours | Serves: 8

1-pound candy coating, chopped	1 teaspoon vanilla
2 cups semisweet chocolate chips	1 cup coconut
1 square baking chocolate, chopped	2 cups roasted peanuts

1. Mix together the candy coating, chips, and chocolate in the pot. Cover and turn the dial to Slow Cook, cook on low until melted, about 3–4 hours, stirring every hour. 2. Press START/STOP to stop cooking. Stir in vanilla, coconut, and peanuts. Drop by teaspoons onto waxed paper. Let it stand until set.

Per Serving: Calories 744; Fat 45. 23g; Sodium 491mg; Carbs 65. 95g; Fiber 6. 8g; Sugar 38. 87g; Protein 24. 11g

Banana Apple Smoothie

Prep time: 15 minutes | Cook time: 0 minutes | Serves: 4

1 banana	1 tbsp stevia
1 apple, cored and peeled	1 cup low fat coconut milk
2 cups filtered water	

1. Add all the ingredients to a food processor, processing until it is smooth. 2. Serve over ice.

Per Serving: Calories 88; Fat 2. 22g; Sodium 227mg; Carbs 20. 34g; Fiber 1. 9g; Sugar 9. 99g; Protein 2. 2g

Minty Cabbage & Grape Smoothie

Prep time: 15 minutes | Cook time: 0 minutes | Serves: 4

1 cup red or white grapes	½ cup ice cubes
1 cup sliced frozen or fresh peaches	½ cup water
1 cup chopped cabbage	1 sprig of fresh mint

1. Add all the ingredients to a blender or juicer and blend until they become smooth. After that, serve the mixture in tall glasses right away. 2. You may also tear mint using your fingers and serve it alongside the smoothies, but it's not necessary.

Per Serving: Calories 118; Fat 3. 45g; Sodium 16mg; Carbs 21. 42g; Fiber 1. 9g; Sugar 15. 6g; Protein 1. 31g

Lemony Dessert Peaches

Prep time: 15 minutes | **Cook time:** 20 minutes | **Serves:** 4

1 cup canned peaches in their own juices	1 tsp ground nutmeg
½ tsp cornstarch	Zest of ½ lemon
1 tsp ground cloves	½ cup water
1 tsp ground cinnamon	

1. Drain the peaches. 2. Combine water, cornstarch, nutmeg, cinnamon, ground cloves and lemon zest in the pot. 3. Turn dial to Sear/Sauté, set temperature to HI, and press START/STOP to begin cooking. 4. Add the peaches. Bring to a boil, reduce the heat to LO and simmer for 10 minutes.

Per Serving: Calories 17; Fat 0. 37g; Sodium 70mg; Carbs 3. 59g; Fiber 1. 6g; Sugar 1. 71g; Protein 0. 55g

Pineapple Carrot Cake

Prep time: 15 minutes | **Cook time:** 2½-3 hours | **Serves:** 8

Unsalted butter, for greasing	3 large eggs
1 (14-ounce) can sliced carrots, drained	2 cups all-purpose flour
⅓ cup vegetable oil	1 teaspoon baking soda
¼ cup orange juice	1 teaspoon baking powder
1 cup granulated sugar	1 (8-ounce) can crushed pineapple, with juices
⅔ cup packed brown sugar	2 teaspoons vanilla extract

1. Grease the pot thoroughly with butter. 2. Incorporate the carrots, oil, and orange juice into a pot and mash them using a fork. Then mix in the granulated and brown sugar, followed by beating in the eggs. 3. Next, add the flour, baking soda, and baking powder and mix until blended. After that, add the pineapple along with its juices and vanilla, and stir until the mixture is even. Finally, even out the top of the mixture. 4. Cover and turn the dial to Slow Cook, cook on High for 2½ to 3 hours, or until a toothpick inserted into the cake's center comes out with just a few crumbs attached. Unplug the pot and let cool uncovered for 1 hour before serving. 5. Scoop the cake warm out of the pot to serve, or let it cool completely in the pot. Frost if desired

Per Serving: Calories 729; Fat 11. 69g; Sodium 188mg; Carbs 151. 67g; Fiber 2. 4g; Sugar 125. 2g; Protein 7. 13g

Chocolate Brownie Cake

Prep time: 15 minutes | Cook time: 3-4 hours | Serves: 8

10 tablespoons unsalted butter, at room temperature, plus more for greasing	1½ cups all-purpose flour
1¼ cups packed brown sugar	⅓ cup cocoa powder
4 large eggs	1 teaspoon baking powder
2 teaspoons vanilla extract	⅛ teaspoon salt
	1 cup semisweet chocolate chips

1. Grease the pot thoroughly with butter. 2. Mix together the butter and brown sugar in the pot. Add the eggs and vanilla and beat until combined. 3. Stir in the flour, baking powder, cocoa powder, and salt until just combined. Then stir in the chocolate chips and smooth the surface of the batter. 4. Cover and turn the dial to Slow Cook, cook on Low for 3 to 4 hours, or until the brownie is set on top. Scoop out of the pot to serve. 5. Store leftovers covered at room temperature for up to 4 days or freeze for up to 2 months.

Per Serving: Calories 360; Fat 13. 51g; Sodium 61mg; Carbs 56. 71g; Fiber 1. 9g; Sugar 35. 51g; Protein 5. 19g

Delicious Banana Foster

Prep time: 15 minutes | Cook time: 2 hours | Serves: 4

½ cup (1 stick) unsalted butter, melted	4 nearly ripe but firm bananas, peeled and halved lengthwise
¼ packed cup brown sugar	¼ cup dark rum
½ teaspoon ground cinnamon	
¼ teaspoon ground nutmeg	

1. Pour the melted butter into the pot and whisk in the brown sugar, cinnamon, and nutmeg. 2. Place the bananas in the pot in a single layer. Turn to coat them evenly in the butter and spice mixture. 3. Cover and turn the dial to Slow Cook, cook on low for 2 hours, or until the bananas are very tender and the sauce is slightly thickened. 4. Add the rum and mix it well. It's fine if some of the bananas get mashed up. 5. Cover and continue to cook for another 15 minutes before serving.

Per Serving: Calories 331; Fat 15. 88g; Sodium 15mg; Carbs 40. 77g; Fiber 3. 3g; Sugar 27. 78g; Protein 2. 25g

Vanilla Almond–Caramel Sauce

Prep time: 15 minutes | **Cook time:** 8-9 hours | **Serves:** 16

2 (14-ounce) cans sweetened condensed milk	1 teaspoon sea salt
¼ cup almond butter	¼ cup amaretto liqueur (optional) or more almond milk
¼ cup almond milk	4 teaspoons pure vanilla extract, divided

1. Combine the condensed milk, almond butter, almond milk, salt, and amaretto liqueur (optional) in a large bowl and stir until the mixture becomes smooth. 2. Split the mixture evenly between two pint-sized, heat-resistant canning jars with lids, ensuring that there is at least ½ inch of space at the top of the jars. Seal the jars securely. 3. Put the jars into a pot and add enough water to completely cover them, with an additional inch of water above the top of the jars. 4. Cover and turn the dial to Slow Cook, cook on low for 8 to 9 hours. 5. Using tongs and hot pads, carefully remove the hot jars from the water. Set them on a wire rack to cool. 6. Once they are cool enough to remove the lids, stir 2 teaspoons of the vanilla extract into each jar. 7. Cover tightly again and refrigerate for up to 3 months. Use some sauce in a recipe, or heat it in the microwave and drizzle over your favorite dessert.

Per Serving: Calories 63; Fat 4. 01g; Sodium 183mg; Carbs 4. 12g; Fiber 0. 4g; Sugar 3. 73g; Protein 2. 55g

Pumpkin–Cranberry Bread Pudding

Prep time: 15 minutes | **Cook time:** 4-6 hours | **Serves:** 8

1 loaf store-bought pumpkin bread, cubed	2 large egg yolks
1 cup dried cranberries	⅓ cup unsalted butter, melted
1 cup canned solid-pack pumpkin purée (not pumpkin pie filling)	2 teaspoons ground cinnamon
	⅛ teaspoon ground nutmeg
1 cup half-and-half	⅛ teaspoon sea salt
¼ cup pumpkin butter	1 cup salted almond-caramel sauce (optional)
½ cup brown sugar	Ice cream, for serving (optional)
2 large eggs	

1. Place the pumpkin bread and dried cranberries in the pot. 2. Mix together the pumpkin purée with the half-and-half in a large bowl, stir until smooth. 3. Mix together the pumpkin butter, eggs, brown sugar, egg yolks, cinnamon, nutmeg, butter, and salt until they form a smooth mixture. 4. Then, pour this mixture into the pot, ensuring that all the bread cubes are fully coated. 5. Cover and turn the dial to Slow Cook, cook on low for 4 to 6 hours, or until a food thermometer registers 160°F. 6. Serve the pudding warm with the caramel sauce and ice cream, if desired.

Per Serving: Calories 524; Fat 33. 39g; Sodium 370mg; Carbs 50. 68g; Fiber 6. 9g; Sugar 23. 14g; Protein 12. 34g

Honey Bananas

Prep time: 15 minutes | **Cook time:** 15 hours | **Serves:** 2

2 large bananas
2 tsp clear honey

1 tbsp coconut cream

1. Turn dial to Bake, set temperature to 350°F, set time to 5 minutes and press START/STOP to begin preheating. Cut both ends off the bananas. Place in the bottom of the pot. Bake for 10-15 minutes or until the banana skins are blackened. 2. Drizzle with honey and serve with a dollop of coconut cream. 3. Sprinkle a little cinnamon over the top of the bananas.

Per Serving: Calories 151; Fat 2. 99g; Sodium 2mg; Carbs 33. 26g; Fiber 3. 2g; Sugar 20. 22g; Protein 1. 58g

Homemade Peanut Butter Chocolate Cake

Prep time: 15 minutes | **Cook time:** 3 hours | **Serves:** 6

1 tablespoon butter
1 box chocolate cake mix
3 eggs
½ cup oil

1¼ cups water
1 cup butterscotch chips
1 cup creamy peanut butter
½ cup milk

1. Coat the inside of the pot with the butter, making sure to cover about two-thirds up the sides of the pot. 2. Combine the cake mix, eggs, oil, and water in a bowl. Pour the mixture into the pot. 3. Sprinkle the butterscotch chips over the surface of the cake batter. 4. In the same bowl you used to mix the cake batter, combine the peanut butter and milk. 5. Top the cake batter with spoonfuls of the peanut butter mixture, dropping each spoonful a few inches apart. Use a knife to swirl the peanut butter mixture, incorporating the butterscotch chips as you go. Make sure not to thoroughly mix. You still want a distinct peanut butter swirl. 6. Cover and turn the dial to Slow Cook, cook on low for 3 hours, until set.

Per Serving: Calories 534; Fat 33. 7g; Sodium 945mg; Carbs 51. 87g; Fiber 1. 5g; Sugar 11. 42g; Protein 9. 21g

Vanilla Chocolate Lava Cake

Prep time: 15 minutes | Cook time: 3½ hours | Serves: 8

1 tablespoon butter	1½ cups water
1 box chocolate cake mix	1 (4-ounce) package instant chocolate pudding mix
3 eggs	2 cups whole milk
½ cup oil	1 tablespoon instant coffee powder (optional)
2 teaspoons vanilla extract	1 (11-ounce) bag 60 percent cacao chocolate chips

1. Coat the inside of the pot with the butter, making sure to cover about two-thirds up the sides of the pot.
2. Mix together the cake mix, eggs, vanilla, oil, and water in a large bowl. Pour the mixture into the pot.
3. In the same bowl you used to mix the cake batter, whisk together the milk, pudding mix, and instant coffee powder. Pour this mixture over the chocolate cake mix. Top with the chocolate chips. 4. Cover and turn the dial to Slow Cook, cook on high for 3 hours and 30 minutes, until set in the center.

Per Serving: Calories 607; Fat 30. 39g; Sodium 1115mg; Carbs 80. 71g; Fiber 3g; Sugar 43. 2g; Protein 8. 59g

Pumpkin Cake

Prep time: 15 minutes | Cook time: 4 hours | Serves: 6

1 tablespoon unsalted butter, plus ½ cup melted	¾ cup brown sugar
1 (15-ounce) can pumpkin puree	1 tablespoon pumpkin pie spice
1 cup whole milk	1 teaspoon vanilla extract
2 eggs, beaten	1 box yellow cake mix

1. Coat the inside of the pot with 1 tablespoon of butter, making sure to cover about two-thirds up the sides of the pot. 2. Add the pumpkin, milk, pumpkin pie spice, eggs, brown sugar, and vanilla to the pot and stir until just combined. 3. In a separate large bowl, combine the remaining ½ cup of melted butter and cake mix until crumbly. Spread the cake mixture over the pumpkin mixture in the pot. 4. Cover with the lid. Turn the dial to Slow Cook, cook on low for 4 hours. Let the cake cool to room temperature before serving.

Per Serving: Calories 484; Fat 29. 29g; Sodium 106mg; Carbs 48. 03g; Fiber 3. 9g; Sugar 32. 28g; Protein 9. 45g

Cherries Stuffed Apples

Prep time: 15 minutes | Cook time: 40 minutes | Serves: 6

⅓ cup dried cherries, coarsely chopped
3 tablespoons chopped walnuts
1 tablespoon ground flaxseed meal
1 tablespoon firmly packed brown sugar
1 teaspoon ground cinnamon
⅛ teaspoon nutmeg

6 Golden Delicious apples, about 2 pounds total weight, washed and unpeeled
½ cup 100 percent apple juice
¼ cup water
2 tablespoons dark honey
2 teaspoons extra-virgin olive oil

1. Turn dial to Bake, set temperature to 350°F, set time to 5 minutes and press START/STOP to begin preheating. 2. Mix together the cherries, walnuts, brown sugar, flaxseed meal, cinnamon, and nutmeg in a small bowl and stir until all the ingredients are evenly distributed. Set aside. 3. Working from the stem end, core each apple, stopping ¾ of an inch from the bottom. 4. Gently press the cherries into each apple cavity. Arrange the apples upright in the pot. 5. Pour the apple juice and water into the pot. 6. Evenly distribute honey and oil over the apples and then bake them for 35 to 40 minutes, or until the apples are soft enough to be easily pierced with a knife. 7. Transfer the apples to individual plates and drizzle with the juices in the pot. Serve warm.

Per Serving: Calories 474; Fat 4. 43g; Sodium 35mg; Carbs 108. 2g; Fiber 12. 1g; Sugar 89. 95g; Protein 2. 74g

Peach Crumble

Prep time: 15 minutes | Cook time: 30 minutes | Serves: 8

8 ripe peaches, peeled, pitted and sliced
3 tablespoons freshly squeezed lemon juice
½ teaspoon ground cinnamon
¼ teaspoon ground nutmeg

½ cup oat flour
¼ cup packed dark brown sugar
2 tablespoons margarine, cut into thin slices
¼ cup quick-cooking oats

1. Turn dial to Bake, set temperature to 350°F, set time to 5 minutes and press START/STOP to begin preheating. Lightly coat the inside of the pot with cooking spray. Arrange peach slices in the bottom of the pot and sprinkle with the lemon juice, cinnamon, and nutmeg. 2. Mix together the flour and brown sugar in a small bowl. Using your fingers, break the margarine into small pieces and mix it with the mixture of flour and sugar. Then, add the raw oats and mix everything together. Sprinkle the flour mixture over the peaches. 3. Bake until the peaches are soft and the topping is browned, about 30 minutes. 4. Cut into 8 even slices and serve warm.

Per Serving: Calories 129; Fat 3. 97g; Sodium 3mg; Carbs 23. 17g; Fiber 2. 9g; Sugar 15. 86g; Protein 2. 54g

Cinnamon Oranges with Raspberries

Prep time: 15 minutes | **Cook time:** 0 minutes | **Serves:** 4

4 navel oranges
2 tablespoons orange juice
2 tablespoons lemon juice
1 tablespoon sugar

½ teaspoon ground cinnamon
½ cup fresh raspberries
4 sprigs fresh mint

1. Firstly, use a sharp knife to peel off the outer skin and the white part of the oranges. Then, cut each orange into 5 or 6 pieces and place them on four plates. 2. Secondly, mix together the orange and lemon juices, sugar, and cinnamon, and pour this mixture over the oranges. 3. Finally, add some raspberries and a sprig of fresh mint on each plate, and serve immediately.

Per Serving: Calories 293; Fat 5. 28g; Sodium 3mg; Carbs 62. 11g; Fiber 5. 4g; Sugar 49. 09g; Protein 2. 33g

Baked Five-Spice Stuffed Apples

Prep time: 15 minutes | **Cook time:** 8 hours | **Serves:** 4

¼ cup honey
Zest and juice of 1 orange
1½ teaspoons Chinese five-spice powder

3 tablespoons chopped pecans
4 sweet-tart apples, cored, bottoms intact

1. Combine honey, orange zest (keep the juice aside), and five-spice powder in a small bowl. Add pecans and mix well. 2. Fill the hollow spaces in the apples with the mixture. 3. Place the apples upright in the pot. 4. Pour the orange juice you set aside earlier over the apples. 5. Cover and turn the dial to Slow Cook, cook on low for 8 hours.

Per Serving: Calories 206; Fat 4. 24g; Sodium 24mg; Carbs 45. 63g; Fiber 5g; Sugar 38. 35g; Protein 1. 21g

Conclusion

The Ninja Foodi PossibleCooker PRO is a versatile 8-in-1 kitchen appliance that can cook variety of meats and vegetables. With this appliance, you can enjoy deliciously fried and baked food while also preparing healthier desserts and snacks. By eliminating excess fats from your food, you can achieve your desired level of crispiness without compromising on taste.

This all-in-one appliance is perfect for those looking to lighten their kitchen workload. With its high-capacity pot, you can easily prepare meals for the whole family in a single batch. The dishwasher-safe accessories and easy-to-understand cooking settings make cleaning and cooking a breeze.

If you're ready to make a healthy lifestyle change and begin your weight loss journey, the Ninja Foodi PossibleCooker PRO, along with its recommended cookbook, is the perfect choice. Start creating delicious and healthy meals for yourself and your loved ones today.

Appendix 1 Measurement Conversion Chart

WEIGHT EQUIVALENTS

US STANDARD	METRIC (APPROXINATE)
1 ounce	28 g
2 ounces	57 g
5 ounces	142 g
10 ounces	284 g
15 ounces	425 g
16 ounces (1 pound)	455 g
1.5 pounds	680 g
2 pounds	907 g

VOLUME EQUIVALENTS (LIQUID)

US STANDARD	US STANDARD (OUNCES)	METRIC (APPROXIMATE)
2 tablespoons	1 fl.oz	30 mL
¼ cup	2 fl.oz	60 mL
½ cup	4 fl.oz	120 mL
1 cup	8 fl.oz	240 mL
1½ cup	12 fl.oz	355 mL
2 cups or 1 pint	16 fl.oz	475 mL
4 cups or 1 quart	32 fl.oz	1 L
1 gallon	128 fl.oz	4 L

VOLUME EQUIVALENTS (DRY)

US STANDARD	METRIC (APPROXIMATE)
⅛ teaspoon	0.5 mL
¼ teaspoon	1 mL
½ teaspoon	2 mL
¾ teaspoon	4 mL
1 teaspoon	5 mL
1 tablespoon	15 mL
¼ cup	59 mL
½ cup	118 mL
¾ cup	177 mL
1 cup	235 mL
2 cups	475 mL
3 cups	700 mL
4 cups	1 L

TEMPERATURES EQUIVALENTS

FAHRENHEIT(F)	CELSIUS(C) (APPROXIMATE)
225 °F	107 °C
250 °F	120 °C
275 °F	135 °C
300 °F	150 °C
325 °F	160 °C
350 °F	180 °C
375 °F	190 °C
400 °F	205 °C
425 °F	220 °C
450 °F	235 °C
475 °F	245 °C
500 °F	260 °C

Appendix 2 Recipes Index

Made in the USA
Middletown, DE
15 October 2023